A Rainbow Book

Praise for *Hiking the Continental Divide Trail*—

"Jennifer Hanson's *Hiking the Continental Divide Trail: One Woman's Journey* recounts the author's flip-flop hike in 1997. The passage of time has seen many improvements in the route as well as the information available to trail users; and today's traveler will not be quite so alone. Yet, despite these changes, the themes of water, weather, physical challenge, and motivation are as true now as they were a dozen years ago. Jennifer's story is a good read and a rewarding introduction for anyone considering a venture on the CDT."

—JIM WOLF,
CONTINENTAL DIVIDE TRAIL SOCIETY DIRECTOR

"Written from the heart. An important read before taking on the CDT."

—RICK RUSSMAN,
SIERRA CLUB NATIONAL OUTINGS TRIP LEADER,
FORMER NH STATE SENATOR

Hiking
the
Continental
Divide
Trail

—*One Woman's Journey*—

Jennifer A. Hanson

To the Residents & Staff of Coburg Village

[signature]

Rainbow Books, Inc.
F L O R I D A

Library of Congress Cataloging-in-Publication Data

Hanson, Jennifer A., 1959-
Hiking the Continental Divide Trail : one woman's journey / Jennifer A. Hanson.
   p. cm.
Includes index.
ISBN-13: 978-1-56825-120-2 (trade softcover : alk. paper)
ISBN-10: 1-56825-120-3 (trade softcover : alk. paper)
1. Hiking—Continental Divide National Scenic Trail—Guidebooks. 2. Continental Divide National Scenic Trail—Guidebooks. 3. Hanson, Jennifer A., 1959—Anecdotes. I. Title.
GV199.42.C62H36 2011
917.8—dc22

2009024083

Hiking the Continental Divide Trail: One Woman's Journey
© 2011 Jennifer A. Hanson

www.HikingtheCDT.com

ISBN-10: 1-56825-120-3
ISBN-13: 978-1-56825-120-2

Published by
Rainbow Books, Inc., P. O. Box 430, Highland City, FL 33846-0430

Editorial Offices and Wholesale/Distributor Orders
Telephone: (863) 648-4420 • Email: RBlbooks@aol.com
www.RainbowBooksInc.com

Individuals' Orders
Toll-free Telephone (800) 431-1579 www.AllBookStores.com

First Edition 2011

15 14 13 12 11   7 6 5 4 3 2 1

Printed in the United States of America.

To my parents, Don and Lois Hanson, for encouraging me to become the woman I most wanted to be, and for your examples of determination, courage, integrity and kindness.

To my loving partner, Denise Watso, whose belief in me has never wavered. Thank you for a decade of laughs and love as we navigate through life's challenges, together.

To our precious children, Noah and Eliana, who fill my life with joy. May you pursue your dreams with gusto and abandon.

Contents

Contents

Third Leg: From Warm Springs, MT north to Canadian Border

Fourth Leg: From Warm Springs, MT south to South Pass, WY

Fifth Leg: From Silverthorne, CO south to Chama, NM

Map List

Foreword

There are few treasured landscapes that can compare to the Continental Divide National Scenic Trail. More than 3,000 miles in length and passing through five states, the Trail connects some of the most iconic scenery in the West; transports us back in time through history and gives us glimpses of nature in its rawest form.

The highest and wildest of the long trails in this country, the CDT still represents a great challenge to those who attempt to hike it end-to-end, but since the author's epic journey, many improvements have been made. With the formation of the Continental Divide Trail Alliance in 1995, thousands of volunteers have dedicated themselves to the hard work necessary to construct mile after mile of high-quality tread. Thanks to their efforts more than 2,000 miles of the Trail now stand completed.

These volunteers are often transformed by their experiences on the Trail, developing a sense of stewardship for our public lands that is reflected by volunteering in their local communities when they return from the CDT. Many of our passionate volunteers devote part of their vacation every summer to building the Trail. Besides the personal bonds that are formed among our volunteers, there is also the bond with the land and a sense of ownership and pride in the knowledge that their work will enable future generations to enjoy this recreational treasure.

The transformational power of the Trail can even be felt on a short day hike. Looking out from a vista on the Great Divide, reconnecting with the natural world, and sharing these experiences with family and friends is a welcome break from our hectic lives. Introducing young people to the magic of the CDNST is the best way to inspire the next generation of outdoor recreationists and maybe even the next thru-hiker to be. For many, the knowledge that the Trail extends not just around the next ridgeline or peak, but ultimately on north to Canada or south all the way to Mexico is a powerful image that drives the imagination and opens the door for exploration and personal challenge.

Trails are formed by those who use the land, charting their way to some destination: food, water, safety, shelter, vistas, adventure, challenge, change. The National Trails System was designated in 1968 and amended several times since to guide the creation of major trails throughout America such as the Continental Divide National Scenic Trail. This system of long-distance hiking trails is the envy of outdoor recreationists around the world and allows modern-day explorers to enjoy vast stretches of our public lands. In this book, Jennifer Hanson takes us on one such journey and major themes emerge where the physical paths of the trail weave so tightly with her personal paths that neither we nor she can separate one path from the weave of all paths. Thru-hikers take pride in hiking their own hike. Their experiences on the Trail often guide their future life journeys. Can one really separate the winsome song of the chickadee, an elk's bugle ringing through a high, lonesome valley, or the power of a granite thrust piercing the cobalt blue sky from the human longings that well up in us when we confront nature on its own terms—wild and beautiful and punctuated by days of solitude on the trail?

Along the trail Jennifer explores her place in nature and the important connection of women to the wild lands. She explores the weave of her own individuality with the paths of her relationships. She takes us along as she begins to hike her own hike—or is it learning to live her own life?

I meet countless people, not just thru-hikers but hikers of all levels, who can remember vividly their moments of inspiration while on the Trail and who recount for me the transformational effects on their lives of such experiences. Business executives who have turned their companies towards environmental stewardship. Young adults who point their careers to conservation. Teachers and Girl Scout leaders who become committed to helping the children of our nation connect with our wild lands. A past District Governor of Rotary International who is so inspired by the transformational experiences of two Youth Corps volunteers helping to build the Trail that he sets out on his own thru-hike to endow a Youth Corps crew for the Trail. Sometimes I feel we should place at every trailhead a sign, "Beware—transformation ahead."

For generations the Continental Divide was a barrier to our westward migration, later it separated the nation that was forming, and now the Trail winding along the arduous path of the Divide, unites us. It unites people to people, communities to communities, cultures to cultures, and individuals to their callings. I encourage everyone to read this book, but to do so a few chapters at a time. Set the book down and get out on the Trail and experience the High Divide. Then read a few more chapters and go back to the Trail. Let the thread of Jennifer's book entwine with your own experiences out on the Trail and weave the pattern of your own life. When you do, send us your own stories and we will put them out on our website for thousands of people to connect with you through their own experiences, their own images, and our mutual commitment to our wild lands and the trails that connect us.

Here at the Continental Divide Trail Alliance the Trail inspires us everyday to develop new strategies to guide its completion. In the past couple of years the Alliance has opened regional offices in New Mexico and Montana to connect us more closely with the lands and people of those states. Our current comprehensive mapping project will provide up-to-date resources to the public to encourage more people to get out and use the National Scenic Trail safely and easily.

As a public-private partnership, the Alliance is a national model for effectiveness. However, some of the toughest miles lie ahead. We invite you to volunteer, become a member or make a donation. While the Continental Divide National Scenic Trail is a resource for all, those who give back find they get the most out of their experiences on the Trail. Visit our website www.cdtrail.org to learn more and get involved.

See you on the Trail,

Steve Dudley, Executive Director
Continental Divide Trail Alliance
February 9, 2010

"The Trail Unites Us."

Hiking
the
Continental
Divide
Trail

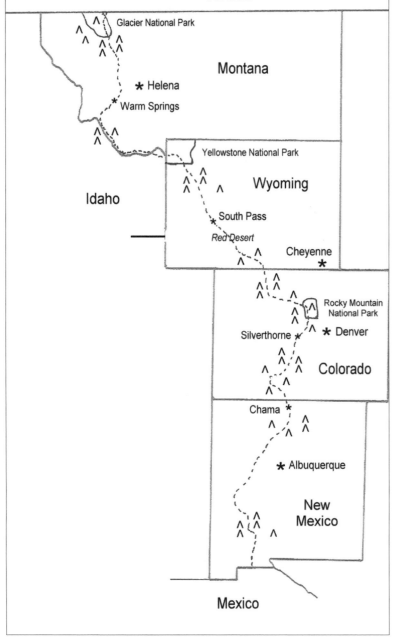

Continental Divide Trail
Mexico to Canada
2,414 miles

Canada

Glacier National Park

Montana

* Helena
* Warm Springs

Yellowstone National Park

Idaho

Wyoming

* South Pass

Red Desert

Cheyenne
*

Rocky Mountain
National Park

Silverthorne *   * Denver

Colorado

Chama *

* Albuquerque

New
Mexico

Mexico

Prologue

It was dusk by the time I reached Big Hole Pass, bone tired from backpacking fourteen hours into Montana's Bitterroot Range. Sleet and now rain had followed me into the mountains, and black water streamed down the trunks of ponderosa pine and Douglas fir. Huddled under a low branch against the weather, I was waiting for a pot of water to boil on my gas stove. I turned on my headlamp and removed the lid from the pot: steam but no bubbles. Replacing the lid, I snapped off the light. The sound of the gas stove was mild comfort as I sat on the damp ground, arms wrapped around my knees, thinking . . .

Though it wasn't uncommon for my husband Greg and I to hike separately, each adrift in our own thoughts, we always came together for dinner; and he always cooked. A sudden ache filled my chest; he was probably at his first stop on his way home to New York. His injured foot had been well enough for him to drive but far too painful to continue hiking the Continental Divide Trail.

The water began to boil. I lifted the lid to my pot and tossed in pasta, freeze-dried beef, and tomato powder. Several minutes later, I turned off the stove and was cloaked in silence; I ate dinner and contemplated my decision to journey on alone. After thru-hiking this past four months with Greg, I could barely conceive of not finishing the last 900 miles. Was I crazy to think I could do it alone?

Alone could easily translate into utter, empty, desolate aloneness — and I was feeling it now. As dinner warmed me, my imagination began to play games with me.

Suddenly vivid in my mind was my seven-year-old self, swinging alone on my elementary school playground, stretching my feet toward the tops of oak trees that rimmed the asphalt.

A classmate came over and sat in the swing next to me.

"I'm going camping," she bragged, "with the Brownies. We get to sleep outside and everything."

I had only a dim idea of what the Brownies were, and I had no idea what "everything" included. After class I ran home and pleaded with my mother to let me "go camping with the Brownies."

"We'll see," she said. It wasn't no, and it wasn't yes, but it was all the answer I was going to get. With eight other children and a tenth on the way she couldn't possibly grant every request. Yet this time, between fixing dinner, doing dishes and changing diapers, she managed to find out what Brownies involved; even better, she signed me up, dug out my father's Army sleeping bag and arranged for him to drop me off at the Girl Scout Lodge that Friday afternoon.

We didn't sleep in the great outdoors — a huge disappointment to me. However, as I lay in the darkened lodge with smoke-drenched hair from an earlier campfire, the clatter of crickets in my ears and the cool night air pouring in through mesh windows, I was enthralled. To me, all the wonder of the woods lived just beyond the end of that enclosed porch.

And so, by the time I was married at the age of thirty-three, I had graduated from West Point and become a captain in the U.S. Army where, among other things, I'd served three years in a high-stress, intensely purposeful, 12-hour-a-day job in Wurzburg, Germany. As a Signal Corps Platoon Leader and Company Executive Officer, each month I participated in week-long field training exercises. Those were the days when Russia and the Cold

War were paramount, and we worked hard to be ready — just in case.

When I was rotated home, however, I found Army life too sedentary. I resigned from the military and proceeded to camp out in all but six states in the United States; I also backpacked throughout the northeast, usually solo, in an effort to get my civilian feet firmly planted on Mother Earth again.

My husband, Greg Allen, and I had met on a trail in western Massachusetts. In the summer of 1994 we hiked the Hundred Mile Wilderness — the final stretch of the 2,166-mile Appalachian Trail.

During those twelve days on the AT, we often camped and hiked with Appalachian Trail thru-hikers, men and women who had spent four to six months walking the entire length of the Trail. We read the logbooks left in shelters, their final entries straining to convey what the summer had meant to them. Their sincerity, humor and courage moved us. Their perseverance awed us. We began to dabble with the idea of hiking a long distance trail ourselves.

By now I had added to my so-called resume. I had spent two years in a cubicle of a Fortune 500 company, been a teacher, counselor and administrator at a retreat center, worked as a ski instructor, looked after children at a home for the severely disabled and monitored the AT for the Appalachian Mountain Club. Meanwhile, Greg was employed by the State of New York as an administrator for the Office of Alcoholism and Substance Abuse Services.

Committing ourselves to a long distance hike would mean putting everything we owned in storage and hiking for six months. Our backpacking experiences had taught us the risks: blisters, sunstroke, hypothermia, lightning, avalanche, river crossings and wild animals.

As our minds wrestled with the idea, our conversation was wonderful to contemplate . . . until I discovered I was pregnant.

Without a second thought, we dismissed the hike and turned to the marvel of parenthood. Then I miscarried. Only then did we reconsider a long distance hike, perhaps this was the only way in which we could escape the shroud of grief that covered our home. And so, in February of 1996, the decision was made, and we began to prepare for a long distance trek.

Chapter 1

Decisions, Decisions, Decisions
15 Months of Planning and Preparation

Though I knew organizing a long distance hike would mean work, I really had no idea. First we had to decide which long distance trail to follow. We easily agreed on the 2,600-mile Continental Divide National Scenic Trail (CDT), a footpath that stretches from Mexico to Canada. We chose it for the adventure it promised.

Remote, inaccessible and with a largely undesignated route, the CDT traverses arid ranchland in New Mexico, the Rocky Mountains in Colorado, the Red Desert and the rugged Wind River Range in Wyoming, and one of the largest wilderness areas in the United States, the Bob Marshall in Montana.

We read in *Backpacker* magazine that only six to eight hikers attempted the CDT each year. And only two or three finished. The statistics thrilled us. With the cockiness of the untried, we were certain we would be successful. Next we had to plan and prepare, and it became a monumental task, consuming nearly every evening and weekend for the next fifteen months.

Though the CDT's remoteness and limited popularity drew us, only short sections of the designated route, a few trails and guidebooks existed. At that time it was actually just an idea of a trail that a handful of others had walked.

Karen Berger and Dan Smith were two who had succeeded. They had written an excellent book about the CDT, *Where the Waters Divide*. We took turns reading their story aloud to one another, highlighting the sections that seemed most relevant to our planning. When we finished, we read it again. After it was drenched on a fishing trip and most of the highlights were washed away, we read it a third time. Then I called Jim Wolf of the Continental Divide Trail Society to order what I assumed to be a full set of maps.

When the boxes arrived we discovered they covered only a third of the distance. Over the next year I ordered dozens of maps from the U.S. Forest Service, Bureau of Land Management (BLM), private companies and Chambers of Commerce for the five states we would cross: New Mexico, Colorado, Wyoming, Idaho and Montana (see Appendix E — Maps). I compiled detailed notes from twelve years of Continental Divide Trail Society newsletters. Finally, I decided to call forest rangers in the areas where our route still seemed unclear.

In the beginning I was nervous the rangers wouldn't take me seriously. I imagined them scoffing at our plans, but they never hesitated. They acted like hiking the Divide was a natural choice, and they rummaged through their maps and memories to give me their best advice. In some cases they went so far as to mail photocopies of their maps with penciled notes, indicating springs and unmarked trails — priceless information — for free.

Using Jim Wolf's *Guides to the Continental Divide Trail*, a few other hikers' routes, and our best judgment, we highlighted our intended trail on the maps, numbering them as we progressed from south to north. It took six weeks to finish a total of ninety-seven maps. By the time we departed for the CDT, we had over 130 maps in all.

Meanwhile, Greg researched the weather we might encounter and new gear we might use. He scanned the Internet for snow pack, temperatures and average rainfall. He researched outdoor cameras, altimeters and Global Positioning Systems (GPS). He ordered stoves and water filters, and returned what wasn't suitable or too clumsy. We each purchased two pairs of boots, one for the desert and one for the mountains. We bought the packs we had always wanted, Dana Design, and ordered trekking poles. We teased each other about looking like gear-nerds, but we couldn't bring ourselves to leave any of it behind.

In the process, we identified thirty-two towns, hunting lodges, ranger stations or homes where we might resupply. In January of 1997, I sent a letter to each of them, asking if we could mail our food packages there, and, if so, what were their hours, and what services were available in their town. We were particularly interested in motels, coin laundries and pizza parlors. The responses were heart-warming. Nearly all replied, many offering encouragement, directions and even home phone numbers.

Next we pondered what food to gather. We rejected the obvious answer of buying the pre-packaged, freeze-dried meals found in backpacking stores. Too expensive. We also chose not to follow the example of many thru-hikers who survive on Lipton Noodles and peanut butter. Instead, we packed a variety of staple items that we could easily combine, were affordable and liked well enough to eat for six months.

Unfortunately, some of our favorite choices turned out to cause the most trouble. The pepperoni and nuts both went bad; and the wax-covered cheese exploded, making a gooey mess of everything it touched. The G.O.R.P (good old raisins and peanuts), Gatorade powder and hot chocolate were too heavy to carry, and the rice cakes were too bulky.

A month into the trip we were leaving half our food behind with a scribbled note encouraging the hotel staff to take it home. But we never left our freeze-dried food.

I had ordered $700 worth of bulk, freeze-dried beef, chicken, brown rice, black beans, lentils, corn, peas, mixed vegetables, hash browns, tomato powder and butter powder. It was worth every penny. After several more trips to a wholesaler, we had a small mountain of food in our spare bedroom.

Twenty-nine resupply boxes packed and ready to be mailed to us along the trail. (Photo: Greg Allen)

With help from friends we spent a week parceling this huge pile into pint-sized bags, filling twenty-nine resupply boxes.

One last step was to find someone to mail our resupply packages to us on the trail. Greg's good friend, Luke Luyckx, was the ideal person for the job. He is an avid outdoorsman and extremely dependable; best yet, he volunteered. In the long run, Luke involved his brother, Chris Luyckx, and Chris's wife, Kathy — they lived in Wyoming — to help us while on the CDT.

Luke's role may not sound like a big deal, but it was. If our supplies didn't arrive at the right place on the right day, we would have been stranded without travel checks, food for the next leg and the maps we needed to continue hiking. To complicate matters we were constantly adjusting our schedule and asking Luke to add or remove items or calling on Chris and Kathy to lend a hand in some way. No question about it, in the end we would never be able to thank Luke, Chris and Kathy enough for their support — all three were just terrific.

Meanwhile, in the midst of our preparations, we tried to get in shape. We borrowed a StairMaster and bought a second-hand weight set. I made charts to track our progress and keep us motivated. My favorite was a poster of a mountain with two hikers ascending from different directions. Each time we worked out on the StairMaster, we moved our hikers up the slope, one inch for every 2,000 steps. It took us months to reach the top. And when we did — it was time to depart.

March 27, 1997 found us loading our car for the long drive from New York to New Mexico. We stopped overnight at my parent's home in Indiana, once in Kansas and again at my sister's house in Denver. Then, on the evening of March 30, we pulled into our motel in a small New Mexico town, Chama, near the Colorado border. We had arranged to leave our car with the local motel owners. In the morning, my friend Stef Fuegi would give us a ride to the Mexican border, 650 trail-miles away.

At the time, Greg's greatest fears about the CDT were bears, lightning and boredom. My only fear was that I would finish the trail and be unchanged by it.

First Leg

From the Mexican Border north to Chama, NM

Colorado

Chama

Jicarilla
Apache
Indian
Reservation

Ghost Ranch
Conference Center

Cuba

Torreon
Trading
Post

Grants

El Malpais
Nat'l Monument

* Albuquerque

Arizona

Quemado

Reserve

New
Mexico

Gila Cliff Dwellings

Pinos Altos

Deming

Columbus

Texas

Mexico

Chapter 2

Hiking at Last
Mexican Border north to Deming, NM

"Smile!" called Stef, poised with a camera to take our picture.

Greg held my hand as we stood in the cool shade of the Mexican Border Station. It was April 1, 1997, and after fifteen months of planning, eight months of conditioning, three months of packing and five days of driving, we were at our New Mexico starting point and anxious to begin our six-month trek on the Continental Divide National Scenic Trail.

As we huddled for that beginning photo, I felt self-conscious in light of the border guards' indifference. Surely they saw only a handful of hikers each year, yet no one stared, no one pointed, they didn't even seem to notice us at all. Maybe they weren't surprised by anything a couple of crazy Anglos might do. I ignored them ignoring us, and in my escalating excitement wished to get on with the hike. Finally, we waved goodbye to Stef and began our walk north on the shoulder of Route 11.

Traffic, though spotty, was fairly steady. It was the only sign of life between the border and our first destination, Columbus, New Mexico, three miles ahead.

The temperature was in the 70s and climbing, the sun unyielding. At 3,990 feet the climate was ideally suited for the prickly pear, mesquite, creosote and saltbush that dotted the dry, flat lands stretched endlessly around us. It was open here, really open, uncluttered by buildings, trees or hills, and it took me some time to absorb the immensity of the place.

The gray Florida (Flo REE da) Mountains rose sharply from the floor of the Chihuahuan Desert, their jagged peaks scraping against a deep blue sky. They were over twenty miles away yet could be clearly seen through the dry desert air. The Tres Hermanes Mountains, an equal distance to our left, offered a brief respite for my searching eyes.

As I grew more accustomed to the subtleties of the landscape, I noticed a small, dark spot rippling in heat waves. Ah, I thought, the Columbus water tower. Feeling halfway there, I began humming a soft tune under my breath and wiggled my toes to forestall any numbing.

Greg walked beside me, his clean, red pack in bright relief against the tans and browns that surrounded us. Though he is dark complexioned, his arms and legs were pale from a long winter indoors. With only sleeveless mesh shirts and running shorts, we were vulnerable to the sun, shrubs and windblown sand.

"We're doing it, Babe. We're doing it," he said for the third time since we had started.

I smiled in return, wondering if he too was having a hard time feeling at home here. New Mexico is as different a place from New York as can be found. It is hot to our cold, dry to our wet, flat to our rolling — a harshly uninviting desert. For a fleeting moment I wondered if our plan to hike the Continental Divide was a colossal mistake. Further, after only a mile of walking, I needed to go to the bathroom — badly.

Because we had driven to the border that morning, what little confidence we had in our ability to find water soon disappeared. With an annual average rainfall of only eight inches, the landscape held little promise. Though we planned to rely on windmills for water, we had spotted only a few of those in the distance, and I was concerned they might not work.

We had taken turns chugging on Stef's emergency gallon of water — just in case. Now I had to solve the problem I'd created.

I looked on both sides of the two-lane road, searching for cover from the view of passing motorists. The ground sloped from the pavement and flattened out just prior to a fence. In that fifteen-foot span were beer bottles and trash, jeep tracks, sagebrush and cactus: plenty to trip over but little to hide behind. Searching ahead, I could see no variation to this except the water tower — taunting us in the distance.

"Can't you wait until we reach town? Thirty minutes maybe?" Greg asked.

I shook my head and hurried toward the fence.

"You're going to go right there in front of everyone?" he called out in alarm.

"Do I have much choice? Anyway, maybe they're not looking at us." As I squatted low behind a two-foot clump of sage, Greg joined me. I was envious that he didn't have to remove his pack to relieve himself.

"It's clear," he announced, telling me the color of his urine. If he were dehydrated, it would be dark. Clear was good.

Finished and feeling better, we returned to the edge of the road and continued north. Somewhere between the first and second mile markers we ran out of things to talk about. I willed myself not to look at the water tower, but there was little else for my eyes to rest upon.

Glancing at my watch, I did a quick calculation of how far we had come, how long it had taken, our walking speed and the time it would take to get to Columbus. Twenty-one minutes. I couldn't have known then how many thousand of times I would convert miles into minutes over the course of that summer.

When we finally arrived in the tiny town of Columbus, we spotted a sign just to the side of the road: Gallery Tea Room. It was down a sandy road — hopefully, an oasis in the desert.

The Gallery Tea Room had a shady courtyard with stone floors and inviting tables and chairs. Encouraged, we opened the squeaky screen door and stepped inside with a sigh. It proved itself to be just as inviting inside as outside. In fact, much to our surprise, it was cooler, nicer there than we had imagined. We sat down at a table and ordered burritos. While we ate, we planned our route to a windmill seven miles northeast. We would leave the paved road in Columbus and follow jeep trails as far as they would take us. After that, we would walk cross-country to the windmill. Hopefully it was there; and, hopefully it held water.

Once we departed the cool shelter of the Gallery Tea Room and the village of Columbus, I was filled with nervous excitement. The sound of traffic faded behind us. The whole world was spread out before me, a mysterious and dangerous world. Best of all, it was wide open and seemingly empty. No would-be advisors lurked in visitor centers or campgrounds. No ranger assured us of water ahead or cautioned us about rattlesnakes. We were alone without coach or critic, utterly free to explore this desert and muster our best resources to overcome its challenges. I felt like the luckiest person in the world.

Soon, though, reality took hold. Sage and creosote bushes crowded our jeep trail, forcing us to walk on the sandy roadbed. The sun thrashed us from a pale blue sky. We made frequent stops — to drink, check our maps, adjust our gear and so on. I was impatient for the soothing rhythm of uninterrupted hiking, but it was as though we needed to ease ourselves deeper into this foreign land before it accepted us.

A mile farther and we stopped again. Sitting in the sand, we checked our feet for blisters, and Greg rubbed the insole of his left foot. Three weeks earlier, after returning from a heli-skiing trip, a pain in the ball of his foot had gotten worse. His podiatrist diagnosed him with Morton's Neuroma, an inflammation of the nerve jacket. He fitted Greg for orthotics, gave him a cortisone shot and a list of specialists along our route.

As I watched him pull his boots back on, I couldn't help but feel I had been right; he shouldn't have gone skiing. The risk of injury had been too high. But I also felt guilty: if I hadn't insisted on receiving the new ski boots, instead of Greg, perhaps he wouldn't have injured his foot in the first place.

Continuing east on the jeep road, a long-eared rabbit suddenly darted in front of us, then just as quickly leaped out of sight. Greg asked me to retrieve the animal guidebook from the hood of his pack, and we identified the black-tailed jackrabbit, a common species in the area. It was buff-colored and sprinkled with black, had unusually long ears and legs, and a black stripe running down its back. The hare had moved so quickly that we weren't surprised to read they could reach speeds of 45 miles per hour and reach heights of 15 to 20 feet in a single jump.

We flushed out several more jackrabbits that afternoon; their sudden presence both thrilled and reassured me. We were doing what we had set out to do, walking through a desert wilderness. Even though a barbed-wire fence surrounded this place, it still contained the wildlife and natural challenges we sought. In fact, because the rancher's cattle ate much of the undergrowth, the black-tailed jackrabbit could more easily spot and avoid predators. In an area mankind had fenced off and claimed as its own, the wild jackrabbit thrived. Perhaps we would, as well.

The afternoon droned on; the warm breeze and dusty scent of sage lulled me into a listless walk. My thoughts were random and immediate. Were the backs of my legs getting sunburned? Which direction was the wind blowing? Could I walk on this clump of grass without twisting my ankle? Look at how quickly that cloud ballooned and then disappeared. Was a blister forming on my baby toe? What's that dark spot on the horizon? A cow!

As the hours passed and I settled into hiking, my thoughts drifted to what we would cook for dinner, what we would do if the windmill was dry, and how many miles we would hike before camping. At last the day waned, and I found myself humming nameless tunes while numbly staring at the back of Greg's boots, relieved of the burden of figuring out where to step next. I can honestly say I was not bored, but perhaps I am more easily entertained than most.

We found the windmill just where the map said it would be. The blades spun lazily in the late afternoon breeze, and near its base was a

large rusty tank that stood a little taller than Greg. He ditched his pack
and climbed on top, scooping water into our bottles. It was warm and
greenish, but it was water.

Lucky us!

We ate dinner in the shade of a crooked-armed tree, anxious to
finish before any cattle arrived at the windmill tank. Their deep footprints
surrounded the stock tank, and their droppings buzzed with flies.

I wasn't altogether certain if it was all right to be hiking across this
ranch, taking water from someone's windmill. We had heard that some
hikers had been charged with trespassing in the area; but that was
infrequent, and the task of securing permission from every ranch we
might cross in this 650-mile state had seemed too overwhelming. We
decided to ask as we passed.

That seemed like a reasonable approach, especially when we
planned the hike from New York. Now hindsight proved us wrong. We
had just spent an entire day hiking on a ranch so large that we never
saw a fence, paved road, truck, building or person. Who were we
going to ask? Maybe we should have written ahead . . . So, as we took
turns scooping stew out of our single cooking pot, our eyes darted
nervously to the horizon; we were searching for the tell-tale dust of an
approaching truck or horse. I wondered if early settlers had felt this
way, constantly looking over their shoulders, never resting their guard.

As night fell, we hiked between irrigated rows of black soil that
stretched a quarter of a mile or more. A brightly lit ranch house illumined
the sky a mile away, and we passed silently to avoid alerting any dogs
on the property.

Exhausted, we set up camp in the middle of nowhere. It was 8:00
p.m. and pitch dark — except for the brilliant light of more stars than
I had seen before. The sky swarmed with the glitter of the Milky Way.

Then there was the drama of the Comet Hale-Bopp, which we saw for the very first time. Though motionless to the naked eye, the comet appeared to streak toward the Earth, a broad white plume trailing behind. Later I would learn that two local amateur astronomers had discovered Hale-Bopp: Alan Hale of New Mexico and Thomas Bopp from Arizona. At the time, however, I simply took its presence to be an omen, a celestial firework meant to bless our journey.

I nestled closer to Greg in my sleeping bag. He rolled onto his side and kissed me in the dark.

"Thank you," I whispered. "Thanks for everything." My words failed to capture all that I was feeling, and I tried again. "I just can't believe we're out here, Greg. I am so, so grateful."

"Me too, honey, me too. Just think. One day down — 184 to go." He laughed as he shifted on his mattress, trying to get warm in a bag too thin for the 30-degree night.

I smiled in the dark, feeling the warmth of Greg's good humor and steady strength, attributes that had forged a deep bond with his brother and mother, close friends, and our two large dogs. His empathy and caring for others had led him to become a social worker; and for all the same reasons, I looked forward to spending the next six months with him.

"Thank you, Lord," I whispered and fell asleep as I wondered at a sky so very crowded with stars it was impossible to take it all in.

I awoke just before midnight and pulled back my fleece cap to see the sky again. A quarter moon hung low on the horizon, drowning out the lesser stars. I spotted the Big Dipper and realized it had spun 45 degrees. Whereas the bowl had opened to my left four hours earlier, it now opened straight down. Whenever I awoke later that night I checked its position, and by the time the sun rose at 7:00, the Big Dipper was turned nearly 180 degrees.

Thrilled with my discovery, I could hardly wait to tell others. As soon as it was light enough to see, I drew the spinning dipper in my journal and later sketched it in a letter to my friend, Naomi Call. I felt like Lewis and Clark, and we had only been on the trail one day.

By afternoon of the next day, we reached the foothills of the Florida Mountains, and my excitement of the morning had long passed. We had hiked over seventeen miles, were sunburned, blistered and low on water.

"The windmill should be this way in 1.2 miles," Greg said, pointing uphill.

Early morning hiking past the Florida Mountains, New Mexico. (Photo: Jennifer Hanson)

The sandy trail snaked through the broad canyon past yucca plants, cactus and long-armed prickly things. I dropped my pack.

Greg glanced in my direction.

I waited for the lecture on setting my pack down gently as Greg cautioned me about "breaking something." Like what? I thought. My sleeping bag? I was more than weary.

Greg just frowned and returned to his map.

"I don't know, Greg. It's hard to imagine a windmill stuck in this tight of a canyon. How would wind get to it?"

"Maybe it opens up —"

"Can't we just use *this* water? You know . . . if we filter it a couple of times?" I nodded toward the stock tank. It was nearly three o'clock, and aside from a pesticide-filled irrigation ditch, the stock tank held the only water we had seen all day.

"I'm not drinking that, Jen. You can, but I'm not."

I walked over to look again. The tank was five feet across and held six inches of rainwater crowded with scum, sand, twigs and what appeared to be pieces of old metal and possibly paint chips. Maybe Greg was right.

With less than a half-pint each, we left the stock tank and trudged up the canyon. I regretted not carrying more water from yesterday's windmill, but at eight pounds per gallon, we couldn't afford the extra weight. If we didn't find water by nightfall, we would go to bed hungry, our freeze-dried dinner inedible.

More importantly, we faced the embarrassing prospect of becoming dehydrated on our second day on the trail. I scanned myself for the early symptoms: thirst, fatigue, nausea and muddled thinking. I was plenty thirsty and tired — but who wouldn't be after hiking all day in the Chihuahuan Desert? I wasn't nauseous, and as for muddled thinking, well, could I really claim to be clear-headed, hiking from Mexico to Canada?

An hour later I climbed out of the sandy stream-bed into the head of the canyon. Sweat stung my eyes as I studied the surrounding mountains: brush, cactus, boulders and sheer rock cliffs. No windmill. No roads.

We took a break under the quasi-shade of a large mesquite bush. Our faces were flush, and we sweated profusely. Greg was nauseated, as well. I was concerned that he was developing heat exhaustion, though the real danger would be if he stopped perspiring and his body temperature rose. According to our first-aid book, the remedy was an ice-cold bath; fat chance of that.

In truth, I was more disturbed by Greg's condition than I let on. In the four years we had been together, he had always been ahead of me with his ever-ready smile and encouraging words: at the top of a mountain, end of a ski run, sinking a basketball lay-up or casting a fishing line. In contrast, his silence now was unsettling.

"Mind if I go look around?" I asked.

Greg grunted.

I left my pack with Greg and headed deeper into the canyon. Why does the GPS keep pointing north? I asked myself. The Global Positioning System (GPS) is a hand-held device that uses satellites to determine the latitude and longitude of one's position. It could also calculate the distance and compass bearing to any other location, in this case, our next windmill.

When Greg first mentioned buying the GPS, I resisted. I didn't want to go on the hike loaded down with technology that was designed to protect us from the wilderness experience we sought. I wanted to navigate using terrain analysis, a simple compass and gut instinct. I feared that if I relied on a computer, my senses would atrophy. But he had his heart set on it, and I grudgingly agreed.

This can't be right, I thought. North would take us over that cliff. Unless we find a trail, we'll be forced to go back the way we came. I scouted east, hoping to find a break in the wall. Nothing. I searched another twenty minutes and was just turning back when something caught my eye . . .

A mountain-biker!

He ripped over the north wall and dipped in and out of my view as he glided into the canyon. Flashing gaudy Spandex, a sleek helmet and water bottles, he sped toward me.

I'll flag him down and ask for water, I thought. Surely this is an emergency. But as he came closer, I just stood there — motionless. Somewhere in the far reaches of my weary brain was the sun-baked thought that he would automatically slam on his breaks, come to a halt and ask if I needed help.

He didn't.

As I watched him disappear into the canyon, I cursed myself. I also felt silly. How can we be dying of thirst while people ride by on bikes? A moment later I realized the obvious. He had come from the north, and he had come fast. He must have been on a trail. I returned to tell Greg, and we were soon on our way out of the canyon.

The top was a narrow shelf of stone and dirt swept clean by a cooling breeze. I studied the canyon we were entering and saw a reassuring dirt road leading northwest toward Deming, New Mexico, the next day's destination.

Greg fought past his growing nausea and hauled his fifty-four pound pack to the top. We headed down. It didn't take us long to reach the windmill and a full water tank, sunlight dancing on its surface. In minutes we were splashing water over our heads and filling our bottles to the brim. Greg's heat exhaustion quickly subsided, and he began carrying additional water to support his greater size, never again suffering from the heat.

We arrived in the town of Deming the following afternoon, checked into the Mirader Motel, took a shower and hurried across the street to eat the best Mexican food we had ever experienced, no doubt enhanced by three days of freeze-dried meals. Back in our room, we sorted through our gear and set aside anything we could do without. Between the heavy weight of our packs and the hard desert floor, our feet were taking a pounding.

Following the backpacker's adage, "If you watch the ounces, the pounds will take care of themselves," I counted out ten small and five large Band-Aids before tossing the rest on the return pile. Next I squeezed half our toothpaste into the trash, then pulled out my compass and stared at it, considering.

"I guess with the GPS, we don't really need two of these," I ventured.

Greg looked up, "No, probably not." He watched as I spun the dial on my dad's old compass. "But, Honey, we could send back ours and keep your dad's," he added thoughtfully.

I looked at the sturdy compass and rawhide string my father had given me and thought of Dad and his battle with cancer. He had received another chemo treatment last week. He was probably at the peak of his side-effect stage. That was when he didn't allow visitors; and that was when the vomiting and weakness overcame him.

I remembered how thin his hands were as he untied the compass from his hunting jacket, saying that he wouldn't need it anymore. The cancer had changed my father, softened him — gave him back some of what he had lost in Vietnam as an Army officer.

Dad had always been a highly emotional man who loved children and enjoyed a good laugh. One of my most vivid memories was on a Mother's Day when Dad began reading a passage from the Bible honoring mothers. To my amazement he was so moved he began to cry and had to pass The Book on for my oldest brother to finish. But three years later he returned from his second tour in Vietnam a different person — angry and harsh. When I wanted to learn Spanish in high school, he said, "Spanish-speaking people are a dime-a-dozen. Take Latin."

Later when I expressed interest in getting a master's degree in English Literature, he said, "The library is full of books. Stick with engineering."

After he visited me at the non-profit teaching center where I had lived and worked for three years, his only comment was, "I wouldn't be caught dead in a place like this!"

He wasn't exactly the first person I called when we decided to take six months to go hiking. When he did find out, strangely enough, he didn't object. A few months later he was diagnosed with lung cancer, caused by the Agent Orange used in Vietnam. After the shock wore off, miracles started to happen.

As a career Army officer, devout Catholic and father of ten children, Dad didn't often indulge in talking about himself or his feelings; but after reading that psychotherapy improved both the quality and duration of a cancer patient's life, he began therapy with Dr. Bill Morice, a psychologist with whom he could relate.

Dr. Morice was an ex-Marine, and my father talked freely of his feelings and eventually opened up to his children in new and profound ways. By the time I visited him in Indiana, months after deciding to hike the Continental Divide, Dad had become one of our strongest supporters.

Before the weekend was out, he had given me his knife, compass and three hundred dollars, saying, "You can work the rest of your life, but you're not always going to be young and healthy enough to do a hike like this. Let me know if you need anything. I don't want you on the CDT worrying about something as frivolous as money."

Now my eyes welled with tears, and I studied the compass in my hands. Though he had given it to me with the intention of being helpful, I had my own compass, one that was smaller, lighter and fit me just right. My father would have been the first to tell me to send his back; still, it seemed sacrilege not to carry my dying father's gift.

I looked past his compass to the palm of my hand, swollen from the rub of my trekking poles. It had only been three days, and already we had been lost, dehydrated and blistered. Just that very morning we sat down for a break only to discover that the ground was covered with tiny, tenacious thorns. I suddenly felt grim.

The more we hiked, the more treacherous it became. Would it all end with one miscalculation of the GPS, a windmill that had gone dry or any of a hundred mishaps? It seemed we couldn't let down our guard for a minute; and I could not afford to carry extra weight for sentimental reasons. My dad would never know; I would never tell . . .

I stepped over to the return pile.

Greg glanced up. "Really, Jen, I think you should carry his compass. It can't be more than two ounces heavier."

"It all adds up." I placed it on the pile. And in the moment I knew . . .

Dad would understand.

Chapter 3

Windmills, Stock Tanks and the Gila River
Deming, NM north to Quemado, NM

Two days later we were hiking along the old Butterfield Stagecoach route through Cooke's Range. I tried to imagine what it was like to travel in the region a century and a half earlier. At that time, Apache warriors roamed the mountains, and places like Massacre Peak, Starvation Draw and Rattlesnake Ridge had earned their names.

The caretaker of the Fort Cummings Historic Site, Doris Kendle, had told us about the pictographs and caves created by the Apaches in the rocky slopes past Massacre Peak. When we reached that area we shed our packs, ate pepperoni and cheese and crackers for lunch, then split up to search the hills.

Though the sun reflected harshly off the rocks, the strong winds and nippy temperatures forced us to keep our jackets and warm hats on. I picked my way among the cool, tan boulders until I heard a shout from Greg. He had found a symbol etched in the stone that looked to be alien: three concentric circles on top of a cross.

Scouring the area, we discovered what we assumed to be an ancient dwelling. Someone had piled stones from the slope to the underside of a massive boulder, creating a dark shelter within. A narrow entrance was open in the middle of the wall.

I sat on a nearby rock while Greg photographed the cave. How had they lived here? I wondered. Where had they found water?

Drowsy from the morning's walk, I stared into space and mused about that so-called "alien symbol" and those early inhabitants. I imagined them as hardened and wily, able to withstand the sun's rays, moving stealthily among the rocky slopes and enduring long periods without water. In contrast, I felt pale, weak and ill-equipped.

Greg came into view, and we headed back down the slope. He told me of the cisterns he had discovered, natural caverns in the rocks that the Apaches used to store water. Soon we rounded a boulder, expecting to find our packs waiting in the sun. They weren't!

Other than the Fort Cummings caretaker, there probably wasn't another person within a 20-mile radius. That ruled out theft. We finally reasoned that our packs were in the next chute; but again the red and green packs were ominously missing.

What if we couldn't find them? How far could we get without water?

Those questions left me cold.

Hurrying on, we crossed the boulder field and rounded the edge of the hill. There stood our packs, just as we had left them. Relieved, we laughed off our rising panic, but we had learned a valuable lesson.

My feet throbbed as we walked our final miles that day. The broad gravel road had grown tedious, and a windmill — our destination — didn't look any closer than it had an hour earlier. I was tired, thirsty and sunburned. Worse yet, a sweat rash had developed on my fanny, rubbing painfully with each step.

Mentally, I began writing a letter to my friend Bethany Gonyea. I began by describing the finest details of the landscape around me: flower petals, whitish-blue sky, clumps of prickly pear and the fiercely rising cold wind. I studied the windmill again, wondering if it really looked bigger — or if my imagination was playing tricks on me.

Continuing the letter in my mind, I told Bethany about my changing prayer life. She would understand. As a Biofeedback Specialist and Reikki Master, my friend of three years was well versed in the growing science of the mind-body connection. Back home, we often called one another and spoke about our lives and spiritual discoveries. Mentally, I wrote . . .

I've noticed a distinct rise in my impulse to give thanks to God. It seems utterly appropriate to thank Him for the water the rancher gave us, for the shelter of the caretaker's trailer, for the certainty of this rocky road. In a way I rarely experience back home, God seems to be the direct cause of every blessing we receive in the desert.

My paragraph ended, and I was plunged into an awareness of my immediate surroundings. The desert wind rushed to fill the void, as unrelenting as ever. According to Ayurvedic medicine, popularized by the Indian physician and writer, Deepak Chopra, I have a "Vata-Pitta" body-type. As such, I am of medium stature, highly competitive, quick, light and aggravated by an abundance of air.

New Mexico wind is certainly an abundance of air. The constant blowing of the past few days had left me irritable and disoriented, and there was no escape from it. No building or automobile to offer protection; no tent to put up or umbrella to erect. I couldn't dash to the store or rummage in the garage to find what I needed. I had only what I carried. Coupled with an imaginative mind and a willingness to try, I could only hope it was enough.

As I picked my way down the gravel road, stepping over the largest, most painful rocks, I wondered if it would make a difference if I raised my hood. Skeptical but willing, I pulled my fleece hat over my ears and tied the hood of my jacket tight against my face. To my delight, it worked. Without the wind gusting in my ears and rushing down my neck, I became calmer.

Such a small thing! What pleased me most was that I had devised
a simple solution from meager resources.

At long last we reached water in Cooke's Canyon. The windmill
formed a black silhouette against the fading orange of the sunset. We
found a break in the heavy shrub and unrolled our sleeping pads and
bags. Dozens of bats from nearby caves silently darted overhead,
devouring the mosquitoes that bred in the open water tanks.

I took off my boots and socks and, leaning against my pack, felt
the luxurious sensation of no longer walking on throbbing feet. Greg was
cooking, and aside from brushing off an occasional mosquito, I rested.

I had done my job for the day — walked my miles, kept myself fed,
watered and reasonably clean, provided shelter and would soon sleep.
Unless I really wanted to find something to worry about, there was
nothing looming over my head: no lawn to mow, bills to pay or people
to please or piss off. I was utterly content as I watched the sky darken
and the first stars appear.

Thank you, God, I found myself thinking.

Yesterday's end-of-the-day thought followed me through the next
day as we reached the banks of the Mimbres River. The tall grasses
and swaying cottonwood trees were soothing after six days of arid
ranchland. The afternoon sun filtered through the branches to land on
sparkling water. Though we still had time to hike a few more miles, we
decided to enjoy the site and camp there.

I sat at the river bank, pumping water through our filter, when the
fluttering yellow-green leaves of a cottonwood tree drew my attention.
I had always loved the cottonwood. I loved it for its splotchy gray-
and-white trunk, the protective sweep of its branches, the trickling
sound its leaves made when rustled by the wind. I closed my eyes
to listen.

Water and sundown – a windmill at Cooke's Canyon, southern New Mexico.
(Photo: Jennifer Hanson)

We had been averaging fifteen miles a day, and though I was dog-tired, I felt good. My sunburn had begun to tan, my legs felt strong, and the few extra pounds I had brought on the trail were quickly disappearing. Though the past week had offered little leisure and considerable pain, I felt more alive than ever. Our days were rich with new discoveries, our minds void of useless worries, and the evolving rhythm of our nomadic life was comforting in its simplicity.

Upon my return from the river, I found twenty or so cattle grazing less than fifty yards from our campsite. They were spotted black and brown on dingy white coats, menacingly long horns protruding from their heads.

"Greg, look!" I called out in alarm.

He stopped what he was doing. "Jen, they're cows. They're not going to hurt you."

"The horns," I told him. "The horns. What if they charge us?"

"They won't charge. They're used to humans. They came for a drink."

I set down the water, never taking my eyes off the biggest cow. He or she was watching us and inching closer with every step. Maybe Greg was right, but he was accustomed to cattle; he grew up near farms. Not me. I had rarely seen a cow without the protection of a fence, and I had never camped with a herd before.

"Do you want me to scare them off? I hate to do that, but if you really want me to, I will," Greg offered.

I nodded.

He picked up a large stick and waved it in the air as he slowly approached the herd. They shuffled and mooed in protest, then trotted off.

Though I could still see them through the trees, I felt safer.

Greg started dinner. He opened two mayonnaise packets and squeezed them into the pot. They melted into oil. Then he added flour and salt to make a white sauce for pasta.

I sat across from him, measuring flour, baking powder, butter powder, nuts, dried fruit and water into a baggie. I was baking bread. We had brought along a BakePacker, which sat inside our pot and enabled us to steam the dough. Though it used a lot of fuel and the results were soggy, it made a tasty snack for the next day's hike.

After dinner and dishes, I lanced the blood blister on Greg's little toe. It had grown steadily, becoming quite large and painful; but it wasn't infected and would probably heal in a week or so. Similarly, the injured nerve in his foot seemed manageable. Greg had whittled his orthotic into a more comfortable shape, which, coupled with the cortisone shot, eliminated most of his pain.

Later I stretched out in my sleeping bag and watched the stars. Hale-Bopp's Comet still dominated the sky. I searched out the Big Dipper and Orion, wishing I knew more constellations by name. It was a shame that I didn't, and this reminded me of how powerful "naming" could be. In the fantasy books I enjoyed reading, whenever the hero or heroine discovered the true name of a wild and powerful beast, perhaps a dragon, they instantly gained influence over its magical powers and were granted safe passage.

I certainly didn't believe I needed to know the names of these constellations to continue safely on the trail, but I felt something was missing. In an environment where cattle and rocks, stars and trees suddenly encompassed my entire world, it was sad to realize we weren't on a first-name basis.

Come morning, we discovered Greg's air mattress had sprung a leak. A thorn had punctured it. Looking around, we saw what we had missed the day before; the riverbank was covered in thorns. The hairs rose on the back of my neck. It was as though the peaceful riverside had lured us into letting down our guard, only to attack us in our sleep. Maybe we needed to know the thorn bush's name, after all.

We quickly ate breakfast, our usual mixture of instant potatoes, pepperoni and cheese, and headed north. For the next two days we

followed the Mimbres River and on April 8 entered the Gila (HEE la)
National Forest. At an elevation of 6,247 feet, ponderosa pine soared
overhead, their needles blanketing the forest floor. It was cooler here, and for
the first time in over a week, we hiked while shaded from the desert sun.

We stopped at the Mimbres Ranger Station, filled our water bottles
and signed their logbook. As was my habit, I browsed the previous
entries, curious to know who was hiking this arid land. John McGrath,
CDT thru-hiker, had signed in just that morning. He had written a
comment, "Looking to meet other thru-hikers," but left no indication
of where he was camping that night.

We asked the ranger about John and were told that he had picked
up a supply package and departed without indicating his route. We
looked forward to meeting another CDT thru-hiker to experience the
camaraderie of our shared journeys. Because the trail is largely
uncharted and attracts only a handful of thru-hikers each year, running
into one another would be unlikely. As it turned out, we never did meet
John and wouldn't come this close to meeting a fellow thru-hiker for over
five months. In contrast, it's rare for an Appalachian Trail thru-hiker to
go more than twenty-four hours without passing another hiker.

Two days later we woke to find it snowing, heavy at first, then
tapering off to sporadic flurries. By late morning it had changed to a
drizzly rain as we hiked into Corral Canyon and confronted the Gila
River.

The waterway was thirty feet across, two to three feet deep and
moving swiftly. It had worked its way through the wide canyon in a
snake-like pattern, and we soon realized the horses and mules that
had carved our trail had taken the most direct route, crossing and re-
crossing the river a half-dozen times each mile.

We abandoned their trail and fought through the thorny shrubs and tall grasses that stood between its bank and the canyon wall. Soft sand tugged at our feet while the steep slope pulled at our ankles. After rounding the bend, our trail flattened until it reached the next crossing of the Gila.

Greg gestured for me to stay put and headed for the west wall of the canyon, presumably to find a better trail. I stepped to the river's edge and watched the muddy water swirl by. Ten minutes passed. I started to shiver, the cold rain seeping inside my rain jacket. I looked for the bright red of Greg's pack, but I saw only the tan, brown and evergreen canyon, capped by low hanging clouds.

Though I knew Greg expected me to wait for him, there was nothing that stopped me from crossing the river on my own. He was the one who preferred to keep his boots dry and go around, not me.

Feeling guilty but excited, I decided to cross the river. In the past week and a half I rarely had the opportunity to make a significant decision for myself, and I relished facing this challenge alone.

I glanced over my shoulder, glad to see Greg was nowhere in sight, then tightened my waist belt, stepped into the river and gasped. It was freezing. Meanwhile, the current pushed at my legs, threatening to toss me aside like a fallen branch. Shocked by the impossible cold and the swift current, I leaned hard against my trekking poles and struggled to maintain my balance.

This might not have been such a good idea, I thought, but continued on. I planted my trekking poles, then slid my left boot forward, until it was wedged securely on the rocky bottom. A burst of cold water splashed my bare thigh. A third of the way across my feet became completely numb, and it felt as though I were walking across the slippery stones on a pair of wooden stilts.

Biting the inside of my lip, I pushed forward more quickly, praying I wouldn't lose my balance. Halfway there, the water became shallower. For several strides it was only six inches deep, then just as quickly the bottom dropped off and rose to my hiking shorts. I tiptoed along the sandy bottom, and I could feel the river current carrying me downstream as I inched ahead.

The rocky bank was just out of reach. I pushed forward with my poles, while struggling to keep myself upright and my pack dry. I inched nearer. Finally, I grabbed the cattails and pulled myself onto the bank.

By the time Greg arrived I had my boots off and was massaging warmth into my feet. He was annoyed with my crossing alone, but I didn't apologize. If he had the freedom to choose his route, so did I. After all, he was my husband, not my father.

I thought about the Appalachian Trail thru-hiker's motto to "hike your own hike." This encouraged people to decide for themselves how they wanted to experience the trail, rather than trying to match speed, mileage or self-established rules. It was a motto with very practical results. If a single standard for successful thru-hiking were allowed to develop, it could lead to bickering, resentments and hikers pushing beyond personal limits; and that, of course, could ultimately lead to injuries and, conceivably, death.

However, when hiking with a partner, especially a spouse, compromises must be worked out. Since we shared our tent, stove and water filter — and relied on one another for safety — it was difficult to establish *my* hike. Now I began to make the effort.

When Greg surged up a hill, I maintained a pace that was comfortable for me and tried not to feel left behind. When I outdistanced him on the flats, I resisted the urge to slow down; instead, I enjoyed the solitude and the opportunity to be the first to discover what lay ahead.

I thought of my father, confined to his rocking chair and oxygen tank, barely able to move. I had spent too many years seeking his approval and fearing his judgments. Now he was dying, and none of it mattered. Perhaps it never had. I didn't want to keep doing the same with my husband. It wasn't fair to either of us. Perhaps by "hiking my hike" I would learn that it was all right to be separate, while being together.

When we next confronted the Gila, we discussed our options and decided to cross as each of us liked. I splashed into the river in my still-wet boots while Greg changed into his sandals. Once on the other side, I wrung out my socks while Greg changed back into his boots. Then we crossed the next sandbar while spindly branches and tall grass slapped against our wet, cold thighs. Over and over we replayed this dreary and dangerous scene.

Navigating one of twenty-eight crossings of the swift and frigid Gila River, New Mexico. (Photo: Greg Allen)

After a brief stop for lunch, we spotted a column of smoke far down the canyon. At first, we guessed it was created by a camper's fire, but after three more crossings of the Gila, we reached its source. It was a natural hot spring.

Someone had barricaded a shallow pool, simultaneously fed by ice-cold river water and the scorching hot spring. We stripped and entered the steaming water gingerly. It swirled with the movements of our bodies, and we quickly discovered its patterns. After reaching a palatable temperature, we lay perfectly still. Wonderful!

Being a stickler for following our schedule, it was unlike me to loudly proclaim, "I'm staying in this hot spring until the rain stops and the sun comes out, even if I'm here all day."

Greg laughed, and the clouds began to lift almost immediately. Within fifteen minutes the rain had stopped, and the sun was shining, at least long enough for us to get out and dry off.

Another two days and we stood at the pay phone on the porch of Doc's Trading Post. The parking lot was empty, and the air was chilly in the early morning. I was calling my mother.

It was easy to picture her walking through the living room to reach the phone on the green desk. Though she is thirty years older than I, we still look remarkably alike — tall and slender with piercing blue eyes, graceful moves and strong legs. I thought of the blue ribbon she had won for being the fastest runner in her eighth grade class, something that rose in importance during those long days of walking. If she had done that, surely I was strong enough to do this hike.

She answered the phone, "Jennifer!" with an exuberance that surprised me. My mother cherishes her children but is by nature reserved and reticent. Raised as an only child by her German mother and grandmother, she is comfortable with solitude and is somewhat of a loner. It was great to hear her excitement.

After chatting for a few minutes, I asked how Dad was doing. She lowered her voice and explained about a leak he had found in his portable oxygen tank. Though uncomplaining, I could hear the fatigue in her voice. She was worn out with worry and the endless task of keeping up with his growing needs. The sadness I felt contrasted sharply with the morning life bursting around me. Sunlight topped the ridge and spilled into the parking lot as birds called out nearby.

Throughout the hike, I drew support and courage from my mother, Lois Hanson. (Photo: Linda Hanson)

She asked about the hike, and I told her about crossing the Gila River twenty-eight times in one day. It came out sounding a lot more fun than it had been, but in the relative comfort of Doc's Trading Post, misery had a blessedly short memory.

As we talked, a dusty red Silverado truck pulling a horse trailer swerved into the parking lot, spitting dust and gravel with its heavy tires. Two cowboys climbed out of the truck and nodded to Greg.

"Well, look, Mom, I better go. We have a lot of miles to do today. We hope to make it to Reserve by Friday. I'll try to buzz you when we get there."

Hanging up, I felt a lump in my throat. I was homesick for the first time since my freshman year at West Point, twenty years earlier. The intensity of my reaction was surprising, and I could only guess that it was caused by my experiences on the trail.

It seemed odd that the simple act of hiking up and down mountains, sloshing through rivers and sleeping outdoors could somehow bring all my feelings to the surface. I don't think I suddenly loved my mother more, I just felt it differently in the same all-consuming way I was beginning to feel everything else. I wasn't hungry — I was ravenous. When my feet hurt, it was torture, and when I finally crawled into my sleeping bag after a long hike, I floated on waves of absolute bliss.

Later that day we carefully hid our packs at the trailhead. Then, unburdened by their heavy loads, we ran up the dirt path to the Gila Cliff Dwellings.

Built sometime after 1,000 A.D. by ancestors of modern-day Pueblo Indians, the simple stone walls continued to stand much as they were constructed. A dozen or so tourists meandered over the dry cliff ledge, peering into dark corners, snapping pictures or catching their breath after the steep climb. Wafts of pine rose from the canyon floor, and the sun beat down on the barren ledge.

We didn't stay long, which was odd since we had anticipated the stop for over a year. Now that we had been hiking thirteen days, though, it seemed doubtful this was where the ancient ones had lived, at least not in the way we typically think of living. They weren't confined to that dry, tiny ledge, captured so neatly by our cameras and brochures. Perhaps they stored food there and slept there during the winter. Now that I was beginning to feel at home in the Gila forest, I couldn't imagine them cooped up on that dry cliff the way most of us lock ourselves away each night.

Instead, I pictured them in the canyons, hunting deer and rabbit among the juniper and sagebrush. They fished along the banks of the Gila River, slept under the blazing stars of the Milky Way, felt the first breeze just after dawn. This is where they lived, I thought, as we headed down the trail to retrieve our packs. What's more, we had been visiting their home every day of our hike.

That evening we spotted our first herd of elk. Greg was ahead of me on the trail and waved me forward. The small herd grazed in a lush meadow, their mud-brown coats and long antlers clearly visible through the pine forest. We watched them for several long minutes, captivated by their wild beauty. The stream that trickled through their meadow called to us even more strongly.

It was 7:30 p.m. We had been hiking nearly twelve hours and dared not stop until we found water. We reluctantly started hiking again, and the elk slipped into the forest.

Once we reached the meadow, I hurried to put up the tent and filter some water. Greg fired up the stove. Only thirty minutes of daylight remained, and I craved reading a few pages of the paperback I carried. If we didn't finish our chores before dark, I would have to put it off until the following night; our batteries were too important to be wasted on reading and writing. Though it would seem that we had all day long to do just as we liked, in fact, hiking took ten to twelve hours each day, while sleeping and eating consumed twelve more hours. At the most we could afford to relax for ten to fifteen minutes at lunch and perhaps twenty minutes each night.

We left the Gila National Forest, re-supplied in Reserve, and continued north toward Quemado. We were scheduled to arrive there the following day and, as the long hours passed, I followed Greg's boots across rock, sand and gravel. The afternoon dragged on and on, and I became too sleepy to pay much attention to the trail. It was about six o'clock in the evening when I slowed and peered into a gully.

Something was wrong. "Where did the creek go?" I asked.

We had been walking on a paved road beside Largo Creek for several miles; now it was nowhere in sight. It must have dried up, and we didn't notice. I looked back, hoping it had just veered from the road.

Nothing.

Scanning the desert ahead, I saw no gully where a stream might hide. I looked in the ditch. No fresh growth on its banks, no fungus on the rocky bottom, no dark sand at low spots. It was utterly dry. We're back in the desert, folks. Jackrabbits and bleached bones, I thought and chuckled.

I removed my pack and sat on it.

Greg did the same. "How are you for water?" he asked.

"Got about half a bottle. How about you?"

"A quarter."

Knowing we didn't have enough to cook dinner, we had to decide whether we would camp here and go to bed hungry or keep hiking.

"How far is Quemado?" he asked.

"Twelve miles." I didn't need to check the map; even in a stupor I constantly obsessed over that sort of thing.

"How far back do you think it is?" He was begging me to think.

"Well, we hit the creek fifteen miles from Quemado. We've been following it for quite a while. Must not be more than a mile back." I unlaced my boots, quick to rub my feet at any opportunity. "I vote we keep going. Sure don't want to hike in circles, do we?"

"Nope! North it is."

We headed out, searching for a windmill, creek, stock tank or ranch house. Nothing. As the miles ticked by, I found myself not wanting to find water, thinking that perhaps we could make it all the way to Quemado instead. That would mean hiking twenty-seven miles in one day when we had been averaging seventeen. In fact, neither of us had ever gone more than twenty-one miles. But we were on a road, three weeks into the hike and headed to fresh burgers and cold Cokes.

Around dusk a Buick stopped beside us, and the driver, a bearded man who appeared to be in his late 50s, asked if we needed a ride. Greg shook his head no and explained that we were hiking the Continental Divide Trail, end to end. We couldn't accept rides. I felt a certain pride in our turning down his offer, but after watching him disappear down the road, I couldn't help but wish I were sitting in his back seat and just minutes from town.

The sun set over our left shoulders, and we trudged on. Dusk became dark, and passing motorists blinded us with their headlights.

My feet began to hurt in new and profound ways. This wasn't just blister pain, though there was still plenty of that. This was a deep ache caused by walking on hard soil and unforgiving blacktop. Though we wore some of the best hiking boots on the market, each step deepened the bruising in the balls of my feet. The ibuprofen I had taken at lunch had worn off, and my blisters cried for relief as they rubbed against worn bandages. Greg insisted that we stop less frequently, fearing we would arrive after the town was closed, and I scoured my mind for some way to relieve the pain.

"Greg?" I called ahead in the dark.

"Yeah?"

"Can we sing a song?" I strained to ask, unconsciously holding my breath with each step.

He slowed down and walked beside me, singing the famous line from "Me and Bobby McGee" about being broke in Baton Rouge and making his way to the train.

Fresh tears came to my eyes as he sang. I joined in with the few words I knew, and when we finished, he sang another tune. My spirits lifted, my breathing relaxed, and I pitched in with some Girl Scout songs. He took his turn with more popular hits, and I led us in a series of Christmas carols. Near the end we were running out of ideas. Pain rushed in to fill the silence, so we sang barely remembered songs with lengthy choruses of "la, la, la."

The lights on the horizon grew brighter, the traffic heavier. Finally, the road ended. We turned right on the highway and limped to the first building we came to.

It was the Largo Inn.

We found the owner at the bar next door, cashing out, her boyfriend waiting in his pick-up. We got a room, and within minutes we were lying on our beds, feet in the air, soles pressed against the cool white wall.

Chapter 4

A Navaho Storyteller
Quemado, NM north to Chama, NM

In our hotel room in Quemado, New Mexico, Margaret from the Quemado Bureau of Land Management (BLM) pointed on our map to the 115,000-acre El Malpais National Monument that we would soon hike through and told us we shouldn't have any problems finding water. Two days later, while climbing over a barbed-wire fence into the El Malpais, we hoped Margaret was right. Stock tanks and mud puddles had gotten us this far, but we had never become accustomed to the gritty taste.

We entered the El Malpais anticipating the spatter cones, ice caves and lava formations of the inactive Bandera Volcano, but we must have been using the back door, so to speak, since there wasn't even a gate in the fence. On the other side of the barbed wire we were greeted by the same old ranchland — flat red dirt dotted with shrub grass, small brush and an occasional stand of pinyon pine.

Around noon it started to snow, lightly at first and not of much consequence. We put on our rain jackets and kept on hiking. Though Greg's altimeter watch showed the temperature to be in the low 40s, there wasn't much wind, and the day felt mild. A half-hour later the snow stopped, and the sun returned. All around us clumps of white sat atop boughs of bright green. The newly washed sage filled the desert air with its crisp aroma.

An hour later it started to snow again — in earnest this time. Large flakes covered our packs and recently donned jackets. Within minutes we couldn't see more than a hundred feet in any direction. Worse, it turned out that the dirt we were walking on was what Greg called, "Freeze-dried clay." It stuck to our boots like Play-Doh, only heavier and much less fun.

I watched Greg sliding and lurching along the trail without complaint. His size-twelve boots must have weighed five or six pounds each, and I was impressed by his stamina and patience.

Early afternoon arrived, and I prayed the weather would improve soon. We weren't carrying a tent with us, just a tarp, eight feet by ten feet. It was big enough to protect us from snow we might sleep on or snow that might fall on us — but not both.

In hindsight it might seem foolish to hike the 650 miles of New Mexico with only a tarp; but with an average annual rainfall of just eight inches, we had decided to swap our four-pound tent for an eighteen-ounce tarp.

We hadn't regretted that decision — well, not yet.

If it didn't stop snowing, we were going to have a wet camp, but in the desert nothing stays wet for long. Sooner or later we were sure to dry out. Our new sleeping bags were another matter.

After shivering through our first week on the trail, we had ordered the warmest, zero-degree bags we could find. Their thick goose down enabled us finally to sleep in comfort; but if they got wet, they would become cold and heavy, and take forever to dry.

By evening the sun had created large patches of bare earth suitable for camping. When we woke the next day the sky was overcast. By noon we were trudging through eight inches of fresh snow. We fought for purchase on the clay surface of the deeply rutted jeep trail, our boots waterlogged and heavy. Within an hour the strain began to show. My right shin tightened painfully.

I secured my hood against the wind and dropped into a meditative calm. I was contemplating the sensations in my body. Starting at the top of my head, my skull throbbed with dull heaviness.

"Just observe," I remembered my teacher saying in his deep Indian accent. I did a mental check up: There was a kink in my neck and tightness in my shoulders. "Just observe," I repeated to myself. Doing my best not to react, I scanned downward past assorted aches and pains — until I reached my shins.

Pain stabbed through my right leg, seemingly doubled by my full attention. I breathed deeply, maintaining my awareness on the tender shin. I tried not to react but to accept the pain and stop fighting it. For several seconds a tearing sensation streaked up and down my leg, then the pain lessened.

I honestly don't know how meditation works. Perhaps I unconsciously adjusted my stride or relaxed my foot, I'm not sure, but as I observed my bodily sensations, the minutes became hours, and my pain subsided.

Greg shows that our tarp was too small to keep us dry during a three-day snowstorm in central New Mexico. (Photo: Jennifer Hanson)

That night we did our best to keep our sleeping bags dry. It was useless. By morning most of our gear was wet, I was limping badly, and we were not having fun. Without seeing the Bandera Volcano or so much as one lava formation, we hiked to the highway and hitched a ride into town. After a night's rest, we rose early and walked to the bakery.

"You're still limping," Greg said.

I nodded. Streaks of pain shot through my shin, and the blister on my right heel rubbed against the strap of my sandal. I was weary and sluggish in contrast to the bright sunny day.

"Maybe we should take the day off," he suggested.

Our plan had been to eat breakfast, then hitch a ride to where we had stopped hiking the day before. Our idea was to walk back to town and maintain the integrity of our thru-hike. If we took the day off, we'd have to skip the make-up miles to stay on schedule.

"No, let's get it over with," was my reply. "Once we get out there, it should only take us about seven hours. We'll be done by three or four this afternoon."

He shook his head. "Jen, I never meant for this hike to become an endurance test. We're both exhausted, our clothes and boots are still wet, my blisters are worse, and you probably have shin splints." Encouraged by my silence, he added, "You know it's kind of a fanatical, black-and-white thinking to say we *must* walk *every* step of 2,600 miles. Why can't it be enough that we spend six months steadily backpacking from Mexico to Canada along the Continental Divide? And if we miss one nineteen-mile stretch because we were wet and cold, not properly equipped and suffering from shin splints, does that really negate the entire hike?"

"But where's it going to stop?" I demanded. "We've just started the hike. How many more times are we going to be tempted to hitch a ride and skip a section?"

We stood on the sidewalk and waited for the light to change. Motorists drove by in their clean cars and clothes. The muddy, sloppy scene of the past few days seemed surreal. Greg took my elbow, and we crossed the busy highway.

Leaving the bakery, we walked to a nearby park and sat on a bench. Greg took a large bite from his apple turnover, then nodded at the building across the park. "If we stay in town, we could visit the Mining Museum," he suggested.

I stretched my legs and felt the sun warm my aching muscles. Even at home I would take a day off work now and then, I thought, and do something fun. We hadn't done anything except sleep, eat and hike in over three weeks — and everyone thinks we're on some kind of vacation. Still I asked, "If we don't stick with it, what are we going to tell people?"

Greg broke into a grin and kissed my cheek. "We'll tell them the truth, that we hiked the CDT, covering 2,600 miles in six months. Most people won't care that we skipped a twenty-mile stretch. But if they do, we'll just tell them we decided to enjoy our summer as well as complete our goal. That we saw great sights, endured many hardships, made smart decisions and were kind to ourselves."

Relieved that we wouldn't be hiking, I wrapped my arms around Greg and kissed him. Then my doubts returned. "I don't know, Honey. Maybe we should just hike it. If we lose this chance, we're never going to be able to say we did a true end-to-end hike."

"Don't worry about it, Jen. Who's going to care?" He crumpled the tissue that had wrapped the warm apple turnover and tossed it in a nearby trash can.

I will, I thought.

He stood up and wandered toward the museum, read the sign at the front of the building, then turned and waved for me. He either hadn't sensed my continued ambivalence or intended to ignore it.

I let it slide. We didn't hike that twenty miles, and sometimes I lie awake at night and remember.

Four days later we slept in an abandoned adobe hut, and I prayed at the small statue of the Virgin Mary we found behind it. Afterward we climbed out of Arroyo Seccion and entered the Navajo Indian Reservation. Sporadic pinyon pine and sage dotted the rocky landscape, swept bare by the relentless wind and sun. The land was unforgiving, and I had difficulty imagining anyone living here. Yet, the dirt road we hiked was broad, and we soon came upon a cluster of trailer homes.

I had read that if we stayed on the roads, we would not be trespassing; nonetheless, I was nervous and half expected a shout of alarm at our presence. All we heard was our pack straps snapping in the wind.

As we neared the end of the road, we saw a man ease his horse from a corral and walk toward us. His two collies were close behind him.

Greg drew him out with a friendly hello and appreciative comments about his dogs. The Navajo stopped about ten feet short of the road, put one hand in his pocket and loosely held the reins with the other. He was probably in his twenties and wearing a heavy leather jacket, white jeans and a dull blue baseball cap.

Navaho sheepherder, south of the Torreon Trading Post, New Mexico. (Photo: Greg Allen)

With a little coaxing he said that he was a sheepherder, heading out to be with his flock. Usually he would check on the sheep every couple of days, he explained in a voice so quiet I had to concentrate to hear him speak, but since it was calving time, he liked to spend most of his days with his flock. He never knew when a ewe would have a difficult birth.

We nodded as though we understood, and Greg asked if he raced his horse.

He smiled and ducked his head. "No, not much. He's not so fast."

A plume of sand swept across the dirt road. The silence spread comfortably between us. I was itching to go, but neither of the men seemed inclined to move on.

"Do you want to hear about the coyote that stole my father's chickens?" the sheepherder asked.

Greg smiled, and even I was willing to stick around and listen.

"My father had a few chickens he kept in that pen over there." He pointed to a small chicken coop surrounded by a wire fence. It was about twenty feet past the front door of his father's trailer. "One night a coyote burrowed under the fence and stole a chicken. So, my father put that railing around the bottom. But still the coyote got in and stole another chicken. So, my father decided he would have to kill this coyote or lose all his chickens.

"He sat out on the porch with his shotgun all night long. But the coyote was too clever for him. He saw my father with his shotgun and did not come that night or the next night or the one after that. Finally, my father said that we must hide from the coyote and then shoot him. We pulled our mattresses onto the roof of the trailer and stayed there all night long, waiting to shoot the coyote. But we did not get a single shot at him. The coyote did not come.

"After three nights of sleeping on the roof without seeing the coyote, my father decided we must have scared him off. So, we pulled the mattresses down and slept in the house. That night the coyote killed all the rest of my father's chickens." The man stood in silence.

"Then what did you do?" Greg asked.

"We quit raising chickens," he said, smiling.

Their utter acceptance stayed with me long after we left the Navajo Reservation. I kept picturing those two men lugging a mattress onto their roof and wondered if, after all that effort, I could have let it go.

Six days later found us on the eastern slope of the snow-covered San Pedro Range. By noon we were walking through the Chama River Valley. To our north rose orange, yellow and tan cliffs, their bases piled high with mounds of stone, their tops flattened into hot dry mesas. Grayish-green hills marked the eastern horizon, and the floor of the valley was filled with sage. We lingered. The toll of hiking almost 600 miles in parched ranchland and snow-drenched mountains left us yearning for the solace of this gentle valley.

Hiking through the beautiful Chama River Valley in northern New Mexico. (Photo: Jennifer Hanson)

We stopped for lunch under the shade of a juniper and heard the call of an unseen bird. I replayed the melody in my head, yearning to recognize it, categorize it and draw closer to this wild creature by naming it. I knew it wasn't a crow, which, aside from bats, had been our most common winged companion.

"Greg, did you hear that? What kind of bird do you think it is?"

He shrugged and imitated its call. The bird responded in kind. Greg whistled again, and I tried as well. The bird answered once more. Had it sent us a greeting? Were we talking to the bird? One couldn't help but wonder.

Before leaving, I tossed a few peanuts on the rocks behind me. "Thank you, little ones," I called out, and I imagined the delight of the bird or mouse that would discover them.

In the afternoon we reached the Ghost Ranch Conference Center, where we planned to stop and resupply. Crumbling golden cliffs towered over the modest buildings and dirt roads of the facility. Green fields of alfalfa and clover marked the reach of their sprinkler system. We hurried up the mile-long driveway; we were eager to reach the cold sodas we were sure to find there.

Our room was filled with sunlight and sparse furniture: twin beds, a dresser, shelf and straight-back chair. No fancy pictures on the wall or carpet on the floor. It felt like camp, and I loved it.

We stripped, then Greg took our clothes to the washing machine on the other end of the veranda, a towel wrapped around his hips. I sat on the bed closest to the window and opened my mail: ointment for my shins from my friend, Naomi, a letter forwarded from Grants, New Mexico, a pamphlet from our minister and a package from Mom. She wrote:

I suspect that many of these cookies will arrive smashed but crumbs will taste just as good as whole cookies — so enjoy!

Received and turned in two more rolls of film today & they will be back tomorrow afternoon. You are getting some good pictures.

My parents had offered to process our film throughout the summer, creating duplicate copies: one that was returned to us on the trail, the other kept safe with the negatives.

"This way," my father said, "you will be able to critique your picture-taking while giving you a chance to improve your photo abilities along the way."

As for me, I just liked looking at the pictures and forwarding them to friends and family.

Mom's letter continued:

So many of the flowering trees are in full bloom now along with tulips and creeping phlox, etc. Such a pretty time of year.

In addition to keeping us apprised of Dad's condition and the daily activities of her grandchildren, nearly every one of my mother's letters contained some mention of her natural surroundings. Two weeks earlier she told me she had gotten in the first of her garden: radish, onion, spinach and beets. Last time she had written it had been:

The dandelions are so thick in the side yard it's a solid carpet of yellow.

It struck me that living in a ranch house in rural Indiana was also living close to nature. Mom didn't need to hike across the country. She already knew the names of things.

After reading my mail and eating a half-dozen cookies, I limped to the community shower, the concrete floor pressing painfully against my bare, swollen feet. Hot water gushed over my head and shoulders as a steady breeze blew in through the open door.

I thought of Georgia O'Keeffe, the famous woman painter; she had lived and worked at Ghost Ranch in northern New Mexico for many years. The gift shop was filled with books about her life and pictures of her paintings. I could imagine why she had moved here from New York so many years ago — drawn not only by the incredible beauty of the area but by the big, open spaces, the dryness that cleansed the air, and the sun that left bones white and bare.

I marveled at the bravery of women such as O'Keeffe, pursuing careers and living independently during a time when that was scorned. My grandmother, Frances Flugge, had moved from a small town in Wisconsin to San Diego, California to work in the Navy shipyards during World War II. She was accompanied by a girlfriend, her 12-year-old daughter (my mother) and her own mother (my great grandmother). I love to imagine them in California; their daring inspires me during times of doubt.

The next morning, May 6, we packed quickly, stopped at the office to mail a package to Luke and followed directions into the Carson National Forest. After crossing an open field of wild grass, we found a sign on our trail giving the distance to Box Canyon: one mile. We checked our maps, wondering if we were truly headed into a box canyon, or if this was an over-dramatization for the tourists' sake. We decided to stick with the trail; and with the cockiness of thru-hikers, we figured if we reached a box canyon, we would just climb out of it.

Twenty minutes later, sheer cliffs rose 200 feet over our heads, boxing us in, as promised. We laughed at our arrogance and explored the cool, shaded canyon. A thin waterfall cascaded down one wall, landed in a clear pool and fed the stream we had followed to its base. Boulders covered the canyon floor, and our necks ached as we searched for their origin.

Looking up, I shouted, "Hello . . ." Then I listened with satisfaction to the echo of my call. Greg did the same. Delighted, we continued shouting until we grew weary of the sound of our voices responding.

We headed back up our trail. Before long a steep slope of crumbling limestone and loose rock replaced the northern cliff. Careful not to climb too close lest we kicked rocks onto one another, we pulled ourselves up the canyon wall. A half-hour later we collapsed on its rim, sweaty, scratched and shaken by our near falls. But the view of the surrounding canyons with their multicolored cliffs and rich, green bottoms refreshed us. We pulled out our GPS and map, determined our compass azimuth to a distant spring and set out once again.

Heat rose in waves off the sun-scorched plateau, and we knew our brief respite at Ghost Ranch was over. We were back on the trail, a term no longer limited to an established footpath. "Established footpath?" I said to myself and smiled. There wasn't much of that in the wilderness of the Continental Divide Trail.

As so often happened after returning to the trail, we encountered a situation that demanded our full attention.

A rattlesnake blocked our path on a narrow ledge!

I had never seen a live rattlesnake before, but there was no mistaking the distinctive clatter of its vibrating tail. Its head weaved to the left and right, its tongue darted toward Greg's bare leg.

"Stay back," I warned, my eyes never leaving the tan-and-black snake. Its color a nd pattern blended so well into the surrounding rocks that we might have stepped on it had it not alerted us to its presence.

We searched for a way past, but the ledge seemed far too narrow to chance it, since we weren't sure how far it could strike. We looked behind us and saw only the grueling cliff we had just ascended. We could climb farther and go around, but that seemed like a ridiculous amount of work for the sake of one lone rattler.

By now Greg had the camera out and was inching closer for a better shot. The snake lifted its head higher, the rattling intensified.

"Greg," I warned, but he continued to move closer; he was now within eight feet of those poisonous fangs. "Please," I pleaded. He took another step forward. "What am I going to do after it bites you?" I demanded. I was angry now.

That stopped him. He took the picture and backed slowly away.

My heart was racing, but at least we had a better sense of how close we could get without the rattler striking. After watching it a while longer, Greg carefully edged past it, and I quickly followed.

We steadily gained elevation as we hiked across Mogote Plateau, passing herds of more than twenty elk as they grazed in meadows still littered with patches of snow. At 9,000 feet we reached the snow line and plowed through the wet, heavy mess for the better part of two days.

The end of the second day found us seated under a fir tree, legs covered with our tarp, waiting out a snowstorm. Without a tent we couldn't camp because our sleeping bags would get soaked.

I watched the snow land on the tarp, melt and trickle down to the small pool forming above my ankles. Bored, I retrieved my notepad from the hood of my pack and began a letter to my friend, Naomi:

Thank you so much for sending the essential oil. It beat us to Ghost Ranch, and I've been using it. My shin is doing better — slowly.

Greg especially liked your suggestion that we exchange foot rubs each night. For the first time ever, I let him rub between my toes. Did I tell you he wants me to become a massage therapist? No surprise there.

I know you said to soak our feet whenever we get the chance, but its soooo cold, I just can't do it. Does it count if I hold them over a stream and visualize the water washing away the pain?

Here Greg asked, "How long has it been snowing?"

I wrestled the sleeve of my rain jacket off my wrist. "Thirty-five minutes."

I watched the puffy flakes gently fall on the tarp and thought about Naomi. We met at a yoga class she was teaching in her home and soon became friends. We spoke on the phone or chatted after class, kept up with each other's lives. Even so, the busyness of work and families prevented us from connecting as fully or frequently as we wished.

Strangely enough, the hike seemed to change that, at least for me. Though I rarely reached my friends by phone, the time in town being too short and hectic, I frequently wrote long letters, pouring my heart and thoughts into the pages. The act of writing, especially by hand, brought out the very soul of communication, allowing us to connect more deeply than we ever had before.

This became extremely important to me. As the hike progressed and our daily activities became routine, I yearned for meaningful connections with other human beings. My connection with Greg was profound but limited to one person, and anyone we met along the trail was basically here today and gone tomorrow.

For the next six months I was emotionally and spiritually sustained by a steady stream of letters addressed to "General Delivery, Jennifer Hanson. Please hold for CDT Thru-hiker."

Greg interrupted my letter writing, saying, "Did you hear that?"

I scanned the gray sky, peering through the thick snow for the low rumbling that came from the south end of Mogote Ridge. It sounded like an airplane, but I couldn't imagine someone flying in these conditions. It clearly wasn't an avalanche because the hills weren't that steep. It must have been thunder.

We sat in a cloud of swirling snow and fog, waiting. The rumbling came again, closer and louder. Will this day ever end? I wondered. Now on top of worrying about hypothermia, I was counting the seconds between the lightning flash and thunder.

Eighteen seconds; that was about five miles away. Thirteen seconds, three miles. Seven seconds, two miles. Three seconds, too damn close.

Greg reached behind his pack and pulled out his metal trekking poles. Still sitting, he flung them as far as he could. I did the same.

A streak of lightning cracked through the air in the meadow before us. I recoiled into my rain jacket.

"That was close!" Greg sounded scared. He hated lightning more than anything, probably from years as a competitive bass fisherman always exposed on the open water. He had told me of fishing partners who wouldn't leave the water until their poles were humming with electric charge.

A bolt crashed into the pine grove behind us, and we both flinched. I wondered what it would be like to be struck by lightning. Would I know what had happened before I lost consciousness? Would I wake up hours later, face up in the snow? Or would I wake up at all?

Concealed by gently falling snow, the next strikes crashed to our right and in front of us. I could smell ozone in the air, and we sat like frightened rabbits: listening, smelling, watching.

Our situation reminded me of a story in my church magazine. A man and his nine-year-old son were caught in a blizzard. He was unable to find his way in the blinding snow, and they burrowed into a haystack for warmth. Throughout their long stay, he repeated the Prayer for Protection taught in our church. Days later they left the hayfield, unharmed.

I had recited this prayer every week at Sunday Service but had never taken it seriously. Struggling to remember the words, I silently said the "Prayer for Protection" by James Dillet Freeman:

The Light of God surrounds Us.
The Love of God enfolds Us.
The Power of God protects Us.
The Presence of God watches over Us.
Where ever we are God is! And all is well!
Amen.

I didn't feel immediately safe and protected, but at least it distracted me. Tucking my notepad under the tarp, I pulled my knees tight to my chest and repeated the prayer. Each time I finished, I started again. Eventually, I found myself breathing more easily.

The thunderstorm continued pounding the ridge, but it seemed all right now. The worst had passed. After about twenty minutes the thunder stopped and so did the snow. We rose from our cramped positions and shook out our tarp and rain jackets.

Greg fired up the stove and cooked dinner, freeze-dried rice and lentil beans. Gone were the days of elaborate sauces and stove-baked bread. Our packs were too heavy, and food was the biggest culprit. A single pot of boiled rice and lentil beans was typical fare by now. After dinner, we settled into our sleeping bags, our feet still damp and cold but no longer numb. They would be warm by morning, I knew from experience. Greg reached over and traced the outline of my fleece cap as it curved from my forehead to my ear.

I sighed and leaned into his hand.

"Honey, we can't keep doing this," he said.

Reluctantly I agreed. We had been lucky this time, but what if the snow had never stopped? What if it had rained all night? It wouldn't take much more than this for one or both of us to become hypothermic. Hell, we could even die of exposure up here.

In a few days we would reach the town of Chama and pick up our winter gear, including our snowshoes and tent. Then we could be more aggressive. For now, though, we must head off the mountain and hike along valley roads.

Two days passed. We hiked over the final hill into Chama and for the first time got a full view of the Colorado Rockies looming over the town. The mountains were covered with a ten-foot base of snow among the pine and aspen forest. Above the forest were cliffs topped by an unbroken snowfield. The craggy peaks were gray and white with exposed rock and ice, 13,000 feet above sea level.

I remembered a year earlier calling Jim Wolf, Director of the CDT Society. I asked if he thought there would be much snow in the San Juan Mountains when we reached Colorado.

"Absolutely," he told me, "and it'll stay until late June."

"So how do people get through? Snowshoes? Skis?"

"They don't," he said. "They either skip them and come back after the snow's melted, or they start their hike later in the season."

I didn't like his answer, so I asked someone else.

"No way. I wouldn't think of hiking the San Juans in early June," said Carol McVeigh. She and her husband, Joe, had completed the trail a few years earlier and created a video titled, *A Journey on the Divide*. To avoid the spring snow in the Rockies, Joe and Carol had chosen to start later in the summer and hike from Canada south to Mexico. They had no personal experience of snowshoeing through the mountains but told me of someone (a fellow named Dan) who had.

Dan had started his hike on the Mexican border in early April, just as we had; by late May he had reached the Colorado border and contemplated these same mountains. Determined to hike straight through, he called home and had his snowshoes express-mailed to Chama. Then he set out to complete the 170 miles of the San Juan Mountains. He fought his way through deep drifts and narrowly missed being swept away by avalanches. After three weeks Dan was held up in his tent by a vicious snowstorm. When it ended he headed straight out of the mountains and didn't return until every snowflake had melted.

Having seen it all with our own eyes, we were convinced — and it was the perfect place to do it. Our car was in Chama.

Yes, we would leave the Rockies for now, stop in Denver for a couple of days at my sister's house, drive north to South Pass, Wyoming, and leave our car with our friends in Lander. The second leg of our hike would include the only other area free of snow this early in the year, the Red Desert in the Great Divide Basin.

The next morning we checked out of the motel and drove to the crest of Cumbres Pass. I leaned forward and easily picked out the route I would take: past those boulders, up the gully, hop on the ridge and coast to the peak. My legs twitched. In spite of the warnings I yearned to leap from the car and hike straight through the Rockies to Canada.

"I'll be back," I said. "I'll be back." The deep hush of the slopes was comforting. It was as though they heard me and were content to wait for our return in the fall.

Second Leg

From South Pass, WY south to Silverthorne, CO

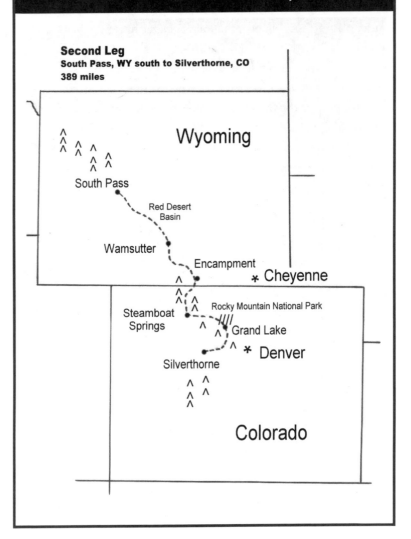

Second Leg
South Pass, WY south to Silverthorne, CO
389 miles

Wyoming

South Pass

Red Desert
Basin

Wamsutter

Encampment

✳ Cheyenne

Steamboat
Springs

Rocky Mountain National Park

Grand Lake

✳ Denver

Silverthorne

Colorado

Chapter 5

Crossing the Red Desert
South Pass, WY south to Encampment, WY

It was May 14 when we spent our first night in Wyoming's Great Divide Basin, home of the Red Desert, an extension of the Great Basin Desert. I was awakened by coyotes barking. They were close — and annoyed. Using our headlamp, I spotted three sets of yellow eyes about twenty-five feet up the slope. I turned off the light and pulled my trekking poles closer. Though I had never heard of coyotes attacking humans, I knew they could take out a deer, and I wasn't much bigger!

We were camped at the only spring in a fifteen-mile radius, and the animals were probably trying to scare us away from a nearby den. In spite of that, I fell asleep quickly and dreamed of coyotes chasing me on the ridge . . . Come morning, I looked for signs of coyotes, but I found none on the hard-packed ground.

We had camped at Edmund Springs at the base of the towering Oregon Buttes. The hills sloped up from our campsite, the red earth etched with deep gullies created by long-forgotten storms. I had asked our hosts in Lander, Chris and Kathy Luyckx, Luke Luyckx's relatives from back home, how a group of hills in the middle of Wyoming came to be named for the state of Oregon. Chris said that early travelers on the Oregon Trail had named the hills because they marked the eastern boundary of the vast Oregon Territory.

I listened as the wind rippled through the stubby grass and had difficulty imagining anyone there beside us, let alone thousands of pioneers in a wagon train. The prairie that stretched east of the Wind River Range seemed empty and desolate. But, of course, it wasn't.

Within a half hour of hiking we encountered our first herd of pronghorns (sometimes called antelopes). We stood stark still as five of the animals leapt from a hidden gully and sped across the prairie. Just as quickly — they stopped. They stood perfectly still, watching us from a half-mile away. Their reddish-brown hides and white bellies were vibrant against the muted tones of the desert.

They must have sensed we were of little danger and began grazing. As we continued hiking, they darted to another area of the prairie, watched for a time, and then ate once again. We loved their sudden, high leaps, quick turns and abrupt stops — so different and yet so similar to the white tail deer we knew in the east.

By late afternoon the hills had flattened into a seamless expanse of sand-colored earth, broken only by small clumps of sagebrush, greasewood and saltbush. When possible we hiked along a cut of gravel roads that had been built for oil rigs near the desert's center. Having expected to find a cloudless sky, I was surprised to see tall cumulus clouds spread low in every direction. A sailor's rhyme came to mind:

> Mare's tails
> and mackerel scales,
> Make lofty ships
> Lower their sails.

But I didn't spot the mare's tails of high wispy cirrus clouds or the mackerel scales of low hanging stratus clouds. Nonetheless, over the next two days we watched as thundershowers poured and lightning flashed on the hills that rimmed the basin dozens of miles away. At first we were refreshed by the scent of falling rain, but as we traveled farther into the basin, even that evaporated. By our second day in the desert, our thoughts were dominated by two things: the pain in our feet and finding water.

"How much you got left?" I asked Greg. We were seated on a large boulder with our pepperoni-and-cracker lunch before us.

"I have about a quarter of a bottle of the desert's finest hot water," he said and sloshed his bottle to prove it. He sat with his hat low on his head and his bandana draped over his neck, safety-pinned in front to protect him from the sun.

It wasn't that we were totally at the mercy of the desert. On our drive up from Denver we had cached two one-gallon jugs of water every 25 miles across the Great Divide Basin, carefully marking the coordinates on our map. We had easily found our cache the night before and used it to cook dinner, eat breakfast and fill our water bottles for the following day. However, we had underestimated how much we would need. With a little over ten miles to our camp, we were nearly out of water. It was 2:00 in the afternoon with clear skies and a 90-degree temperature.

This is crazy, I thought, and polished off lunch. Crazy, crazy, crazy. I rummaged in my backpack for a science fiction paperback book purchased in Denver. I began to read aloud, while Greg finished lunch. It was so poorly written that I never would have read it elsewhere.

That was the opposite of what my friends had suggested. Naomi had encouraged me to breathe into the "sensations" in my feet. Similarly, Bethany advised me to feel each toe, drawing healing energy up from the earth with my breath. I just couldn't do it. My feet hurt too much. It was no comfort at all to know that most thru-hikers experienced excruciating pain in their feet, at least during some portion of their hike. In fact, quite a few suffer from stress fractures and are unable to continue. Even among those who go the whole distance, many share the experience of their feet remaining swollen and tender for months after leaving the trail.

I knew all of that before heading out, but I didn't know how to avoid it. Instead of breathing into my pain or feeling each toe, as my friends recommended, I took three more ibuprofens and read that lousy book.

Crossing Wyoming's barren Red Desert using water we had cached at 25-mile intervals. (Photo: Jennifer Hanson)

We heard the oil rig before we saw it. Its rhythmic clangor traveled across the desert, stealing upon us soon after lunch. Coming over a slight rise, the rig was far ahead on the right side of the road. Its arm swung gracefully up and down as though it were alive. Behind it was a small building.

Surely that must be an office or shelter for employees, I thought. It was easy to imagine a couple of men seated at a desk in their heavily curtained office. There would be an old Coke machine humming in the corner and a tiny restroom in the back. We quickened our pace.

After some time, Greg said, "I don't see a truck or vehicle —"

"No, but maybe they are dropped off to pull their shift."

"Maybe," he said doubtfully.

By the time we arrived in the near vicinity of the rig, we knew we wouldn't find anyone there — and no Coke machine, either. We prayed we would find water, though. The loud sounds were not coming from the silent rig, eerily pumping, but rather from the single-story structure before us.

We stepped through the empty doorway and were blasted by noise. Enduring this assault, we waited for our eyes to adjust to the dark. As sight returned, we realized that, other than the car-sized pump that sat atop a cement slab, the small building was empty. We searched the cinder block walls for a water faucet. There was none. We returned to the outside, looking for our relief. No water. No spring. Discouraged, we slumped against the building's shaded outer wall. The noise and vibration sought to drive us away, but we took off our boots and closed our eyes, unwilling to give up this refuge from the sun. After a brief rest, we sluggishly put on our boots and set out again.

Though the map indicated there was a spring in three miles, we were not to be so easily deceived. With only eight miles to reach our cache, we left the shady refuge and fell into a grim march.

After a while Greg muttered, "Now that's the most realistic mirage I've ever seen."

Heat waves shimmered above and below a pond about a half-mile ahead of us, making it appear to float on the surface of the desert. "Definitely a mirage," I said, but I couldn't tear my eyes away. I remembered the sensation of having my thirst quenched by truly cold, cold water; I imagined cupping water in my hands and pouring it over my head and neck, washing away the crusted salt and dirt.

"Jen, I think it's real!" Greg said, his voice filled with the awe of truth.

"No way," said the voice of reality, suddenly refusing to believe in miracles. "A pond that size would dry up in about a day out here. It's a mirage." In the past two days, we had seen plenty of instances where heat waves had created what appeared to be blue-gray water in the distance. As we drew closer, however, it had always disappeared.

"I think you're wrong this time, Babe." Greg was insistent.

We hiked on; the mirage remained. Finally, we were there, and it was real!

We approached its watery edge. Enclosed in a wire fence was a long pipe that stuck out from the ground and ended above a rusted cattle trough. From the pipe flowed fresh spring water. It splashed over the side of the trough forming a small stream that continuously fed the pond. Though it looked to be only a couple of feet deep, the pool stretched forty feet by thirty feet and was edged by cattails waving in the breeze.

Greg dropped his pack and climbed over the fence. With a loud whoop, he ducked his head under the water then shook it from side to side. I tossed him our water bottles, and he filled them quickly. Cool water surged down my throat, and I finished the bottle in one long drink.

Unwilling to leave the pond, we decided to camp early and stay the night. We had only one day left before reaching Wamsutter, so we opted to start hiking at four the next morning. Though the additional mileage would give us our longest day — thirty-one miles — we hoped to beat the heat and make it to town by early afternoon.

Everyone knows a desert is surprisingly cool at night. I stepped from the tent at three the next morning, and I shivered. Wearing every stitch of warm clothes in our packs, we hiked down a road so dark that we could barely see each other from two feet away. The stars gleamed overhead in the moonless sky, and we sought to pick out every constellation we knew.

Cradling my trekking poles under my arm, I breathed warmth into my hands and smiled into the dark. It felt good to be out here, hiking across the desert at night, I told myself proudly. My pack was light, and we would be in town by early afternoon. I took a deep breath of the cold air and searched the eastern horizon for signs of a rising sun. Nothing.

Now I drifted into picturing my parents sleeping in their beds a thousand miles away — snug and warm. I hadn't thought of them much since calling home from Lander. There hadn't been bad news, though hearing Dad had written his obituary was unsettling. Perhaps I was becoming more accustomed to our nomadic lifestyle and felt less of a need to anchor self with family and friends. Or maybe it was because this desert was so completely isolated. In any event, I felt more self-contained here than I had in New Mexico, less of a traveler and more at home.

Over an hour later the sky became lighter and a thin band of orange spread close to the ground. We had reached the site of our water cache. There we silently ate our cereal, facing the east. Eyes riveted, we watched as that tiny band of light thickened and spread until the sun's first rays shot onto the desert floor. Now the sun was eager to fill the sky with piercing brightness and show us the way.

Just before noon we turned off the gravel road and followed the power line maintenance road as it headed due south. We were gambling that these would lead directly to Wamsutter, but if we were wrong, we were still headed in the right direction.

Within a short distance we found a small, locked utility shed and beside it three coyotes lying on the ground — dead. They were arranged side by side, legs stretched out as though they were running. Flies swarmed over the bodies, smelly in the day's heat.

I looked all around for some indication of how they had died, but all I saw was the endless sweep of prairie reaching off in every direction. Staring back at the coyotes, I was saddened. It seemed likely that a local rancher had done this to protect his livestock. Was it necessary? I couldn't say. I had no idea what these ranchers were up against, though it seemed inhumane to kill animals, lay them out so carefully and walk away as if their lives didn't matter.

We briefly discussed burying them, though we knew it was impossible. Even using our snowshoes as shovels, we doubted we would make much of a dent in the hard desert floor. Besides, we told ourselves, perhaps whoever left them intended to come back, if for nothing other than their pelts.

We continued hiking.

As the hours passed, I silently followed Greg, consumed by the pain streaking through my feet. They hurt so badly that I was holding my breath and fighting back tears. I didn't know what to do. We had just stopped fifteen minutes earlier, and Greg wouldn't want to stop again. Besides, how was I going to get to Wamsutter sitting on my butt?

I was hunched over my trekking poles, trying to walk on my heels when I thought of what my girlfriends had written. *Feel the sensation. Breathe into it. Draw the earth's energy up through your toes.* They seemed like impossible suggestions. Teetering on the edge of what I thought I could endure, how could I possibly feel it more?

I looked up, wincing at the sight of so much empty land to cross. No animals, fences, trees or buildings offered distraction; no landmarks measured our progress. Panic edged closer, and I knew I had to try.

With my next inhale I imagined the air flowing down my throat, through my lungs, abdomen, thighs and into the balls of my feet. Pain exploded into my awareness. It was sharper and clearer than any pain I remembered feeling, including the six times I had broken a bone. I stopped walking and hunched over, tears smarting my eyes.

Long moments passed as I held my breath and then forced myself to stay with the sensations, while continuing to breathe. After another minute or so, the worst seemed over. I imagined the earth's healing energy coming up from the ground.

Concentrating hard, I drew my breath through one toe at a time. The pain lessened. I stood up straighter and took a deep breath. It swirled in and around the bones of my feet, bringing new streaks of pain but taking away others.

I slowly started to walk. Though I had experienced the miraculous healing of meditation many times before, I was still amazed. My feet felt better. Nervous that it might not last, I continued breathing into the balls of my feet, surrendering, accepting and embracing the pain. It never went away entirely, but at least I could walk without crying.

Three miles short of Wamsutter, we were hiking along a dirt road when we were overtaken by a sudden thunder and lightning storm. We searched the flat prairie for any form of protection and found none. When it became obvious we wouldn't be able to outrun it, we ditched our packs, poles and snowshoes. Then we sat thirty yards away on our tiny, foam pads while huddled under our rain jackets. The fury of the storm overtook us as I silently repeated the prayer for protection:

"The light of God surrounds us, the love of God enfolds us . . ."

Waves of thunder crashed into one another as lightning streaked through the air.

"The power of God protects us, the presence of God watches over us," I mumbled.

By now we lay flat against the ground, hands clamped over our heads. After many long minutes, the center of the storm passed, and we stood up to retrieve our gear. We then saw a second wave of storm clouds coming from behind us, and we hurried to stay ahead of them.

When we topped the crest of the next low hill, we saw power lines blocking our route to Wamsutter. In the empty, flat prairie their towers loomed like skyscrapers. Surely these metal frames will suck the lightning right out of the sky, I thought, and zap us in the butt as we pass. It was then that I noticed the metal-grated cattle guard a quarter of a mile farther.

Shouting into the wind, I got Greg's attention and pointed to it. He studied it for a moment, then shrugged as though to say, "What choice do we have?"

With mud gathering on our wet boots we jogged nervously toward the power lines and cattle guard. Our best hope was to get past them before the next storm arrived. Perhaps because we had been up since three in the morning or were giddy from hiking nearly thirty miles, or maybe because I was just plain scared, but the whole situation seemed ridiculously funny. As we ran under the power lines and over the cattle guard, we laughed like idiots.

We stood in the lobby of the Wamsutter Motel the next day, admiring the handcrafted knife handles and belt buckles of Don Taylor, the owner. We had already paid the bill, and our packs waited for us outside. Then our attention was directed to a pickup truck as it pulled into the parking lot out front.

"Here's Don now," said his wife, Arlena, from behind the desk. "He's the Deputy Sheriff. He can answer the questions you were asking." She nodded toward a thin, older man as he stepped down from the truck.

We went outside to introduce ourselves and explain what we were doing. "Is there water on the county road heading south of here?" I asked.

"Nope."

"Well, surely there are stock tanks, windmills, something."

"Nope."

"Aren't there ranch houses along the road?" Greg asked.

"None to speak of."

"There are cattle down there, right?" Annoyed, I swung on my pack and jerked the straps tight. "We saw some just north of town. If there are cattle, there must be water."

He slid past my question and spoke to Greg, "Nope. You best not hike down that way."

That wasn't helpful at all, and it made me angry. I turned and stormed across the parking lot.

Minutes later, Greg caught up with me. "I got directions out of town." He paused. "What do you think about what he said?"

I grunted, too mad to speak.

Greg waited for me to cool off.

Finally, I managed, "You know, he could have tried to help!"

The heat of the noon sun pressed down on all sides. My anger hardened like beef jerky. It seemed some people just wanted to scare us off the trail, as though after hiking nearly 750 miles, we would simply turn around and go home.

"You know I hate to carry extra water," Greg then said, "but do you think we should?"

"Greg, there were cattle north of town. The map doesn't say it's desert south of here. So, there have to be cattle down there."

He hesitated. "Well, yeah, should be."

"Besides, we're going to be following the 130-year-old Overland Stagecoach Trail. In a couple of days we'll reach Muddy Creek. They must have had water to get all those people through."

"I don't know, Jen." He paused, then added with a smile, "A lot of them died."

"To hell with them," I said. "We're not going to quit. We're going to finish this hike." I raised my trekking poles into the air and stabbed my words into the pale sky.

Greg burst out laughing. "Well, then," he said, "come on, Rambo, this is our road!"

We turned down Main Street, hiked past an empty lot and entered the land of no water. Though we would spend hours filtering with bandanas and clogged pumps, spitting poisoned alkaline water from unsuspecting mouths, and cooking with the gritty taste of Muddy Creek, we hiked through southern Wyoming and kept going.

Four days later we reached the foothills of the Sierra Madre Range. It was May 20· and once again we faced mountains covered with snow.

We followed the 130-year-old Overland Stage Station Route from Wamsutter,
Wyoming east to Muddy Creek. (Photo: Greg Allen)

We weren't sure how far we would get, but we had already hiked all
the snow-free regions of the CDT. Unless we wanted to wait a month
for it to melt, we needed to press on.

A chunk of snow kicked free of my snowshoe and plummeted
down the slope. I breathed heavily as I leaned on my poles and waited
for my strength to return. Directly ahead of us rose Bridger Peak at 11,007
feet. It was unspectacular as peaks go, a modest arrangement of icy boulders
and snow covered slopes, but it was not a simple climb. Between the peak
and us was a large basin. Weary from six hours of snowshoeing, I
groaned. What's more, I could feel the effects of the altitude.

When I read last winter that we could expect to acclimatize quickly
enough to safely gain 2,000 feet a day, I remembered thinking that
wasn't very much. We had climbed 2,000 feet in the first few hours of
the day. Since we felt fine, I couldn't imagine stopping to camp at ten

o'clock in the morning. But another two hours and 1,000 feet had made a difference.

"How you doing, Babe?" Greg asked.

"Out of breath," I admitted, "and a little dizzy. Headache. How about you?"

"Same. Sounds like altitude. Want to stop?"

Finding our way to Bridger Peak in the Sierra Madre Range of southern Wyoming. (Photo: Jennifer Hanson)

"No. We're so close to the peak. If a storm came in, it would crush us. We have to reach the other side. Get down a little. Don't you think?"

He nodded. "Yeah, just wanted to check."

Standing directly in front of me, Greg unzipped the hood of my pack to get the aspirin. The sharp odor of his armpits filled my nostrils, and I lifted to my tiptoes to kiss his stubbly chin.

"Hey, hold still," he said.

Smiling, I waited dutifully and swallowed the pills he handed me. Aspirin, drink lots of water and breathe deeply. This was our mountain mantra to thin our blood at higher altitudes.

We descended into the basin by using our snowshoes like clumsy skis. Then Greg began his cautious trek across the empty chute, warily eyeing the slope above him for signs of avalanche danger. He stopped every few steps to watch and listen. From the tree line, I did the same. A chill ran up my back, and I pulled up the zipper of my shirt. What if an avalanche struck?

The fact that we were utterly alone loomed large. No one had more than a vague sense of where we were. Somewhere between Wamsutter and Encampment was all that Luke knew, and it was an area that included ninety-two miles of prairie, forest and the Rocky Mountains. Suddenly the beautiful, snow-covered slope, one like we had enjoyed skiing countless times before, seemed uncaring and malevolent.

Greg inched closer to the center of the basin. I wanted to call out to him, to hear the sound of his voice, but I dared not. It might trigger a slide.

Suddenly, it seemed foolish to be out here alone, friendless and inexperienced in these high mountains. We could so easily become another of those stories in a backpacking journal — the ones that tell of hikers who do something stupid and the rescue teams that risk their lives to save them.

Wind whistled through the tall pines, swaying the branches around me. I looked up and was stunned by the beauty of it. Sunlight glistened off the pine needles while a sky so blue it appeared purple peeked through the branches. I took a deep breath and slowly let it out, eyes closed.

"The light of God surrounds us," I told myself and began my Prayer for Protection. "The love of God embraces us . . ." Then, at its end . . . "It's going to be all right," I told myself. I opened my eyes.

Greg was now more than half-way across and moving quickly.

Too chilly to wait longer, I started out. My snowshoes slid into his tracks, and without looking up or pausing once, I hurried across the eerie basin.

The far edge of the bowl was a nearly vertical climb of several hundred feet. By the time I arrived there, Greg was inching his way up, stopping to gasp for air between breaking trail in deep snow. I ached to help him, but even if I managed to get around him, I would be worn out within a dozen feet. Instead, I climbed his steps like a ladder and waited quietly at his heels.

After an hour of climbing, we topped a plateau of gently rolling hills, 11,000 feet above sea level. We soon came upon a small stream on top of the snow and tried to make up for nearly six hours of minimal water by forcing ourselves to down two bottles of ice-cold snow melt. I winced at the sharp headache it produced but continued to drink. The pine-speckled slopes glistened white and majestic in the afternoon sun. A fresh wind blew steadily from my left, and I turned to find its source — storm clouds!

They were gathering beyond the western ridge and had been too low for us to spot as we were climbing; but now there was no missing them. Like a cat ready to pounce, the storm closed in on our peak.

I groaned in dismay.

Greg turned to follow my gaze. "We'd better get out of here," he said.

We topped off the water bottles, then turned our backs on the clouds and headed across the plateau. The wind rose steadily as clouds piled up around us. At first it was easy going, but as we came to a rise, I started panting heavily. Counting my steps, I refused to allow myself to rest until I reached fifty paces.

Worried I might be slowing us down, I asked Greg if he wanted to take the lead. He declined. Ten minutes later, I realized he had fallen behind. I slowed my pace, expecting him to catch up quickly. He didn't.

"You okay?" I shouted into the gusting wind.

He shook his head no. When he came closer he leaned forward to say something. I strained to catch his words before the wind snatched them away.

" . . . exhausted . . . hit a wall or something."

"Do you have any granola bars?"

Again he shook his head no. "Ate them." Maybe thinking I hadn't heard, he brought his hand to his mouth and made a chewing motion.

I dug into my hip pouch and handed Greg two granola bars. Beyond his shoulder, I saw the gray clouds moving quickly and directly for us. While he ate, I studied my compass and map. We needed to head northwest across the plateau, then drop due south on the gentlest slope we could find. I set the compass to a new azimuth and tucked my map back into its pouch. "I'm going to take some of your weight," I shouted.

He nodded, granola bar in one hand, dripping bottle in the other.

I pulled the water filter, first-aid pouch and rope from his hood and transferred them to my own. It wasn't much, but it was all I could reach without asking him to take off his pack, and we didn't have time for that.

We set out more slowly than before and took frequent but short rest breaks. I kept a careful eye on both the storm and Greg's progress, my senses alert for any change. It reminded me of infantry training at West Point. As cadets we were taken into the mountains, split into small groups, deprived of sleep, handed a map and compass, and told to avoid being ambushed by the enemy while accomplishing our mission. I had thoroughly enjoyed it then, and though I was concerned for our safety on Bridger Peak, I still loved a good challenge.

Over the next half-hour Greg's strength returned, and I gratefully stepped aside as he went ahead of me to break trail. We moved more quickly and soon passed the summit. The plateau sloped gently downward, the wind tapered off, and we entered the relative calm of the leeward side of the mountain. Looking behind us, we saw the storm clouds hovering over the peak; it was as though we had been playing King of the Mountain. The clouds had arrived, but we were long gone.

At the base of a pine tree we stopped for a much needed lunch. Greg retrieved the stove and fuel bottle from his pack, stored high for easy access. Scooping a pot full of snow, he quickly melted it and poured in a packet of ramen soup.

I wanted to puke at the smell of it. Perhaps the altitude left me nauseous, but we had noodle soup almost every day. The problem was, I couldn't think of another hot lunch that was as light to carry and as easy to make.

Nevertheless, I wolfed down my portion, and burned my tongue on the steaming soup. Once finished, I leaned against my pack and closed my eyes. Bright lights flashed behind my eyelids. Though I knew we had to get going, with each breath I sank blissfully away from those flashing lights. Just one more minute, then I'll go, I kept promising myself — until I fell fast asleep.

Greg's movement woke me, and I listened as he packed the stove. I had seen him do it a hundred times, and I could tell from the sounds he made that he was just about finished.

I opened my eyes, refreshed, and ready to move on.

Chapter 6

Snowshoes in Colorado
Encampment, WY south to Silverthorne, CO

Around noon the next day we entered Encampment, Wyoming, Population 490, or so the sign said. As was our habit, we first visited the convenience store and Post Office before heading to Vacher's Bighorn Lodge.

The sunny spring morning coaxed people out of their homes. Two boys rode by on their bikes while a man worked on his motorcycle. We passed a cluster of men leaning against the porch rail of a two-story wooden building. Peering through the open doors, we realized it was a bar. Probably without even trying, it looked exactly like a saloon from an old western movie.

We found Vacher's Bighorn Lodge just past the café. I stepped into the cool lobby and was greeted by the bear, moose and elk heads that hung on the walls. Not being a hunter myself, I was generally creeped out by such trophies. Yet I felt comfortable in their lobby. The soft couches, magazines and fireplace made me feel at home.

"Can I help you?"

I turned to find a young girl standing behind the counter.

Suppressing the urge to look behind her for an adult, I asked for a room for two. Though I'd never encountered this before the hike, it seemed common for the owner's children to watch the front desk while their parents were cleaning rooms. Arriving early in the day as we often did, we frequently checked in with 12-year-olds.

After doing our town chores, we asked Joella Vacher, one of the owners of the Lodge, for a dinner recommendation. She gave us directions, probably not remembering that we were on foot. Ironically, I felt self-conscious walking on the side of the highway without my pack. We were in civilization here, and I wondered what the passing motorists thought of us in the growing dusk. But the food at the Bear Trap Restaurant was delicious, and the two-mile walk was well worth it.

Later, I wrote my mother and confessed:

I'm sitting here stuffed with chili dogs, chips and salad. I'm waiting for my stomach to digest a little of it so I can eat the cheddar cheese popcorn and six remaining oatmeal crème pies that are here next to me. I can hardly wait. We were so hungry on this last leg. We didn't quite run out of food, but we rarely ate our fill.

I doubt she was impressed with my diet, but after hiking 835 miles in seven weeks, my body's metabolism was taking over. The heavy weight of food prevented us from carrying more, and once we reached a town, I couldn't seem to stop eating.

After a two-day rest, we left Encampment and hiked back to the Divide. As we climbed through the foothills of the Sierra Madre Range, our trail was lined with budding aspen and a clear, cascading stream. Bright green cabbage grass and tall daffodils grew beside the waters, and clover-filled meadows stretched down the mountainside. But our brief encounter with spring ended much too quickly. An hour later we reached the snow line and once again donned our snowshoes. Fresh powder fell through the pines, covering our hoods, packs and sleeves.

By six in the evening we were exhausted, but setting up camp in the deep snow seemed more of an effort than continuing to hike. So we moved on. Finally, an odd sight brought us to a halt.

The top of a road sign was sticking up through the snow; only
eighteen inches were visible. Greg lumbered around the front of the
sign to see what it said.

I was too tired to care; I waited patiently, shivering where I stood.

"Wyoming State Line," he read. "We're in Colorado, Jen!"

I smiled in spite of my fatigue. It had been over ten hours since we
reached the snow line, and we had only stopped hiking once. Around
noon we had discovered a picnic site with an unlocked outhouse. We
stuffed our packs into the men's room and sat on the cement floor of
the women's room, free from the wind, and cooked ramen noodles on
the lid of the toilet stool. An appropriate place, I might add.

Meanwhile, Greg's foot was acting up. His Morton's neuroma had
been quiet for most of the hike, but after three days in snowshoes, it
was starting to flare. Snowshoes are designed with a metal plate with
crampons directly below the ball of each foot. This gives the hiker a
secure grip on ice. But with every step, Greg's body weight was pressing
his injured nerve into this steel plate. He was limping badly.

He had told me of the pain early that morning, and we had done
what little we could for the situation. He took three more ibuprofen,
and we transferred some of his gear to my pack. We changed our
route to follow an unplowed road, and I broke trail for much of the day.
In reality, he had little choice but to gut it out.

After setting up camp and cooking dinner, we sank into our sleeping
bags. Though it was too dark to see one another, I gently massaged
Greg's foot, ignoring its moldy odor.

"I think we should consider dropping off the Divide," Greg ventured.
"We busted our butts today on pretty easy terrain and made only 18
miles . . . By the way, that massage feels heavenly."

Though I didn't want to leave the mountains, I knew he was right.
We only had enough food for five days. If we didn't make better time,
we would run out before we got to Steamboat Springs, an option
neither of us was willing to consider. "Yeah, let's do it," I said. "Besides,

Snowshoes were essential in northern Colorado, but their steel plates aggravated Greg's injured foot. (Photo: Jennifer Hanson)

maybe it'll be spring in the valley. I would love to see trees with leaves and grass and flowers. Wouldn't that be wonderful?"

"You crying, Babe?"

"Just a little." I placed his foot gently back into his bag and fell back against my pillow. "I love being out here, Greg, you know that. I love the mountains and the desert and struggling every day to make our miles." I sighed. "But remember when we were leaving Encampment? Remember the aspen we hiked through, and the flowers and little stream beside the road?"

Greg squeezed my hand, and I wiped away a tear. "It was just so gentle and easy. Do you realize those were the first leaves we've seen in nearly two months? It's almost June, and we've only had that one hour of spring. Sometimes I feel like this hike is a weird kind of punishment we're putting ourselves through."

Greg wrapped his arm around me and pulled me close, "I know, I know. But it'll be all right. You're just tired, and we've been pushing hard these past weeks." He pressed his mouth close to my ear and whispered, "Tomorrow we'll leave the mountains and find you spring in the valley — with leaves and grass and a little stream. I promise."

It took two days for Greg's promise to come true. Walking on the shoulder of a paved road, I delighted in the sight of pastures, horses and flat wooded lots. Greg had stopped limping soon after taking off his snowshoes the day before, and we were making good time as we hiked into civilization. A cluster of buildings stood by the road about a mile ahead of us.

"I'm still betting on a convenience store," I said as our debate continued. "See that porch out front?"

"I don't know, Jen. There's no one parked there. Whatever it is, it looks closed."

"No, remember there was that car when we first saw it." I glanced at my watch. "I bet they are open 'til six p.m., and it's twenty of six. If we hurry, we'll get there in time."

Moving more quickly than we had in days, we drew close to the Steamboat Lake Outfitters. It was open until 7:00 p.m. Inside, a few tourists browsed the leather cowboy hats, lassos, wildlife photographs and other upscale items. But we were on the prowl for candy bars, ice cream and cold sodas — and they had plenty of them.

Later, as I checked out the bookrack, I overheard Greg speaking with a man in the next room. I joined them, and Greg introduced me to Don Markley, the owner of Steamboat Lake Outfitters. He appeared to be in his early 50s with a healthy mix of gray and brown in his short-cropped hair. With one hand resting on the glass counter, he listened intently as Greg told him of our hike.

Behind Don hung a framed photograph of a mountain lion looking down on us — ready to pounce. I tensed when I saw it. After nearly two months of living in the wilderness, the threat of the cougar felt more real than the frame that held its picture. My connection with nature had been heightened, and even while indoors I was acutely aware of the wind pushing against the building, instinctively noting the moment a passing cloud blocked the sun's rays. In contrast, the walls, floors, shelves and merchandise seemed terribly artificial and exotic.

"Do you have a place to camp tonight?" Don asked. We shook our heads and said that we planned to stop up the road a couple of miles. It was too early to quit.

"Well, most of what lines the road from here to Steamboat Springs is private land. Finding a place to camp may be difficult," said Don. "But if you don't mind stopping a little early, I know the owner of the fields around here and could get permission for you."

We hesitated. This was new information. We had become so accustomed to pitching our tent wherever we found ourselves that the notion we were on private land and couldn't camp was foreign.

"Where is this place?" Greg asked.

Don directed us out to the porch. His friend's pasture was on the far side of the road. "See there?" he said as he pointed to a stand of trees in the pasture. "You can camp there. I'll call my friend tonight."

Greg glanced at me; I shrugged.

"Well, if you're sure he won't mind," Greg said.

Back inside Greg pulled his money from a Ziploc bag. "How much do I owe you for the bars and sodas?"

"They're on the house," Don replied kindly. "Consider it my donation to your expedition."

Greg looked up, startled. "That is about the nicest thing anyone has done for us, Don. Thank you very much."

Like Greg, I felt moved by Don's offer. We had been on the trail for nearly two months, and this was the first time a stranger had gone

out of his way to help us. Don's generosity was as healing as the
spring grass and yellow-green leaves.

Over the next ten days, we hiked across northern Colorado by
traversing the valleys and snowshoeing over the high mountain passes.
By not continuously hiking along the Continental Divide at the crest of
the snow-covered mountains, we were gentler on our feet, got ahead
of schedule and gave our morale a much-needed boost. After
snowshoeing over 10,180-foot Buffalo Pass, we were hiking through
a valley north of the Rabbit Ear Range and had set up our tent in an
open pasture.

"What's that?" I whispered. Greg lay motionless in his sleeping
bag, listening to the sounds outside.

"A cow?" he asked.

Soon I fell asleep, the strange sounds mingling with my dreams.
Dawn broke on a gorgeous spring morning. As usual I sat in the tent
packing our sleeping bags while Greg took down the rain fly.

"Jen, there's a cow out here," he called out.

I shrugged. We had been camping and hiking and sleeping with
cows most of the past two months.

Then he said more urgently, "Jen, I don't think it's a cow. I think
it's a bull."

I spun around and peered through the mesh of the tent. A hundred
feet behind me stood a full-grown Black Angus bull. It was looking our
way, and it was watching us, but it wasn't terribly bothered by our
presence. It was unusual to find a bull in an open range like this. They
were normally kept in pastures of their own behind sturdy fences and
gates. This one must have gotten loose. We watched the bull and the
bull watched us, and then Greg absentmindedly lifted the rain fly and
snapped it dry.

The bull charged.

Still fifty feet away, he slammed both hooves into the earth and shook his head, snorting and pawing the ground.

He was ready for a fight.

Greg wasn't; he dove back into the tent. Belly down, we watched through the mesh to see what the bull might do.

Still agitated, the bull continued stepping left and right as he bellowed out the strange sound from my dreams. Eventually, the black beast lowered his head and returned to grazing. We waited for him to drift out of sight before packing. He wasn't "drifting" very fast, and I sure wasn't going to go out there and hurry him along. The sun rose; the tent got warmer. A half-hour passed.

"I don't think he can see us if we stay crouched down like this," Greg said.

Though it wasn't easy to put on our backpacks and hike crouched down, we managed to do so as we tip-toed around the bull.

That afternoon we stopped in a field of bright yellow dandelions and prepared to enter the town of Rand, Colorado. We didn't like to offend shop owners with our smelly bodies, so we dabbed a little deodorant on our armpits and brushed our teeth. I don't know how much good it did, but we tried.

Before leaving, Greg arranged the camera on his pack for a delayed photo of the two of us. I felt an impulse to pose as I usually would — seated next to Greg with my arm in his, head cocked slightly with a soft smile; but I didn't this time. Perhaps I was too tired to move the few feet that pose would require, or maybe two months on the trail together had created a closeness that didn't require us to be arm in arm for every photo. There was also a part of me that reveled in being a Continental Divide thru-hiker, and I wanted this photo to capture the strength in me, as well as in Greg. I stayed seated a few feet away, my tan arms loosely wrapped around my knees — my gaze steady and calm, my head erect. The picture tells a story of contentment and confidence.

By skipping lunch we made it to Rand by two in the afternoon. A passing motorist had told us Rand had a convenience store, and we preferred to arrive in town hungry.

Rand included a dozen or so buildings spread along the paved county road. It was quiet — too quiet. We had passed the first few buildings before realizing we hadn't seen a single car or person. Homes and businesses alike seemed locked up or abandoned.

A quarter of a mile into town we saw an old, black car parked facing the street. Painted in bold white letters was "Rand Police" and inside it were seated two men. We headed over to inquire about the convenience store. But by the time we reached the vehicle, we realized the policemen were stuffed dummies, propped up in a patrol car watching for speeders. Like who? Jackrabbits?

We snapped a few pictures, waved goodbye and headed to the far end of town. We had seen a sign and were sure it was the convenience store. To our dismay it too was locked up with lights out. Cursing our luck, we noticed a sign that read, "Closed on Tuesdays." We had to mentally backtrack through the past week to figure it out, but, yes, it was Tuesday.

We bought several sodas from the outdoor Coke machine and sat on the porch. I drank mine too fast and bubbles rose up my nose.

"Where is everybody?" Greg asked.

I shrugged. It gave me the creeps too, but I wasn't in any rush to leave. It had been two days since we had sat in the shade of anything. This could have been the porch of a morgue, and I probably wouldn't have cared. I took off my boots and socks, and leaned against my pack, eyes closed.

"Someone's coming," Greg said.

"Who?" I asked, not opening my eyes.

I waited while he tried to figure it out.

"An ice cream truck! And it's pulling up behind the building. Must be for a delivery." He grabbed my arm. "Give me some money. I'll see if he can sell us some." I tossed Greg our Ziploc bag wallet. He enjoyed few things more than ice cream; I was sure he would be successful.

Wearing unlaced boots he shuffled around the end of the building and soon returned with a half gallon of rocky road and a fist full of quarters. With fresh Cokes, we set the ice cream on the porch and scooped chocolate and nuts into our mouths.

"He couldn't sell us any smaller size," Greg mumbled around a mouth full of ice cream.

I shrugged. "This is great."

Without taking a break or saying another word, we ate the entire half-gallon and licked the cardboard box clean. Securing our packs over full bellies, we picked up our poles and headed back into the sun.

The road east of Rand was lined with tidy ranch houses and fenced pastures. Normally we liked to be securely back into national forest or BLM land before using the "restroom." But I couldn't wait; my bowels churned, and I broke into a sweat.

"I gotta go!" I shouted and dashed behind a row of bushes beside the road. I was surprised to find Greg already dropping his shorts not more than ten feet to my right. It was a long time before I stood up again. Weak and shaking, I walked back to my pack.

"Want some more ice cream?" Greg teased.

I declined to answer.

The next day we crossed 11,200-foot Baker Pass — and with leaping bounds on our snowshoes, slid into the Rocky Mountain National Park. We camped with thousands of starving mosquitoes, forcing us to wear wind pants, long-sleeved shirts, 100 percent DEET and stuffy mosquito net hoods. It wasn't that we were unaccustomed to bugs on the trail — we generally swatted and scratched almost as much as we walked — but this colossal horde of mosquitoes was something new and pretty much beyond belief.

We ate dinner by sneaking spoonfuls of food through the neck opening of our head nets and later brushing mosquitoes off each other's clothes before diving into our tent. Even so, we had more than a dozen of the pests trapped inside. We tried to kill them without smearing their blood — recently our blood — on the walls of the tent.

"After all, we don't want to attract bears with the scent of fresh kill," Greg said with a smile.

During the cool hours of early morning, we escaped from our campsite, crossed over the Colorado River and headed south toward Granby.

Four days later we emerged from the trees above the Saint Louis Creek Valley. Before us was a half-mile of exposed slope ending at the top of the ridge. White bundles of clouds drifted lazily on a sea of dark blue. For the first time, the entire horseshoe ridge of the Saint Louis Peak was visible; its snow-covered arch encircled the valley below.

It was June 5, and a soft rain had fallen all morning, rendering the slope slick and more than dangerous.

"Do you want some water?" Greg asked.

"Huh? Oh, yeah, sure," I mumbled and reached for the bottle. "How's your foot doing?"

"It hurts," he said, and we looked down at his black leather boot, firmly strapped into his snowshoe and covered with chunks of icy snow.

"Dull ache?" I queried.

"Yeah, but now it's starting to give me shooting pains."

"You haven't had those since you were skiing last winter, right?" I looked at him and saw two distorted images of myself in the reflection of his sunglasses. "Honey, could you take off your glasses for a second?" He lifted them, and I saw concern in his eyes.

"You're right," he admitted. "It hasn't hurt this bad since before the steroid shot in March."

"Maybe it's time for another shot? It's been nearly three months."
He lowered his shades and turned to climb higher. "Maybe." He slammed his snowshoe into the icy slope.

I watched as he progressed higher, one kick after another. Finally, I followed.

An hour later we stood perched just below the top of the mountain. Sweating and panting, we bent over our poles as we fought to gain our breath. A vertical wall of snow ten feet high blocked our way. Craning our necks from left to right, we studied the ridgeline on both sides; we were searching for a break in the cornice. There was none. This looked as good a place to climb as any.

Greg glanced over his shoulder at the tree line far below. If we slipped now, we would be in big trouble. He removed his sunglasses, and squinting, studied the cornice as it stretched down the ridge.

"I just hope this snow is strong enough to hold our weight," he said. Greg took a deep breath and turned toward the cornice, hesitated and turned back.

I could tell he was nervous. So was I.

"Give me a kiss for luck," he said.

I took off my sunglasses and kissed him firmly on his snotty, chapped lips. "I love you, Greg." I didn't want to be melodramatic, but I was suddenly consumed by a glaring reality. If something went wrong, this might be the last moment we shared.

Greg nodded as though he had read my mind and then thrust his trekking pole into the wall. It sunk a foot but held steady. Good — so far. After plunging his other pole high into the wall, he thrust his snowshoe into the bank.

Gingerly pressing down, he shifted his weight. It held. Standing atop that shoe he punched another step with his left foot. It collapsed a half-foot — then stopped. I began to breathe again as he continued up the wall.

Actually, it was starting to look like fun. For a moment I was jealous of his going first, breaking trail on this virgin wall. Then it occurred to

me that I didn't have to be jealous. I could do the same. I didn't have to
follow him.

Walking well to the right of Greg, I approached the wall. Heart
racing, I took a furtive look over my shoulder, and a voice inside me
shouted, "This mountain's steep!" As Greg had done, I thrust my
poles and then my snowshoes into the cornice. Not slipping, I took
several steps as though I might be climbing a ladder.

Greg glanced at me. "Hey, you should follow me. It'll be easier for
you."

"Okay. I just wanted to see what it was like," I said and took another
couple of steps. By now I had come level with Greg. I watched as he
struggled to get a steady purchase in the snow and realized my lighter
weight kept me more on top of the powder — an unexpected advantage
of being smaller.

Climbing onto the top of the cornice, I stepped away from the
edge and spread my arms wide. Wave upon wave of snow-covered
peaks of the Colorado Rockies spread before me, while patchy clouds
hung poised in the deep blue sky above me.

It felt incredibly satisfying to be on top, and as so often happens in
the wilderness, the danger and struggle of climbing the mountain quickly
faded in my memory. Now I was simply here. My breath quieted, my
muscles regained their strength, and we could see our destination at
the base of the mountain: Silverthorne, Colorado.

Third Leg

From Warm Springs, MT north to Canadian Border

Chapter 7

Lost!
Warm Springs, MT north to Canadian Border

The Warm Springs, Montana, Greyhound Bus Terminal was primarily a gas station with a convenience store, restaurant, bar and pool tables. The only thing missing was a Post Office. We pulled our packs from the bus storage compartment and leaned them against the building.

It was June 28 and almost three weeks since we had left the CDT at Silverthorne, Colorado. We had spent most of that time in Indiana for my family reunion, and then extended our stay to be with my father in the hospital. He had been admitted with pneumonia days after we reached Silverthorne, and then he was moved to long-term care when the cancer reached his brain. Family gathered, my mother got the rest she had long needed, and doctors gave Dad two to six weeks to live.

With my mother's encouragement we decided to return to the trail until it was closer to his time. With over 1,200 miles remaining and snow likely by early October, we needed to keep hiking if we hoped to finish this year. It was difficult to leave, but we weren't doing anyone much good hanging around the hospital. Besides, as my mom suggested, Dad would have wanted us back on the trail.

I gathered my hiking clothes and went inside the bus terminal convenience store in Warm Springs, Montana, to change. The store was cool and dark, the tiny restroom located to the right of the pool table.

Inside I sat on the toilet for a long time, listening to murmured conversations from the bar. My thoughts drifted to my last night in Indiana.

My father had been agitated all day, rarely lucid and arguing with us all. By evening he was worn down, and I took him in his wheel chair for a stroll in the hospital garden. Stroking his shoulders with one hand as I pushed with the other, I began to sing an old song I learned while in a Christian youth group:

Everything will be all right,
Just lean your thoughts toward the light.
The bad times never last,
Think of Him, and soon they'll pass.

Why don't we trust in the very best?
For all the people needing rest?
The bad times never last,
Think of Him, and soon they'll pass.

Repeating the simple verses, I watched as his shoulders relaxed. "What do you say we mosey on over to the other side, Dad?" He didn't answer, so I wheeled him past the parking lot and up and down the mostly empty lot on the far side.

Unexpectedly, he spoke.

Leaning closer, I asked what he said.

"Are you enjoying your hike?"

"Yes, Dad, very much so. It's as wonderful as I thought it would be." This was the first time in three weeks that he had mentioned it.

I hurried to think of something to hold his interest. "We've been carrying the Gerber knife you gave us the whole way."

He brushed off my comment, mumbling that his son-in-law, Hank, had given the knife to him.

"Then I thank both you and Hank," I said.

He fell silent.

I pushed him past the end of the hospital, beyond the Emergency Room entrance.

Knowing I was leaving the next day and this was probably the last lucid conversation I would ever have with my father, I searched for anything left unsaid between us. Nothing came to mind, though I suppose much could have. I think I was so surprised by the opportunity that I didn't take advantage of it; instead, I asked the first question that came to mind.

"What do you think will happen after you die, Dad?"

"How the hell should I know?" he grumbled, sounding like his old self.

"No, I guess what I mean is — are you afraid to die?"

"No," he said and relaxed. "I'm not afraid to die. I got quite accustomed to the idea when I was in Viet Nam. My only regret is that I won't see my grandchildren grow up."

Tears smarting my eyes, I thought of the children Greg and I planned to have. "Dad, would you do me a favor? After my children are born, will you visit them in their dreams so they know their grandfather?"

After nodding several times, he whispered hoarsely, "If I can."

By the time I kissed him goodbye the next morning, he was completely withdrawn and silent. Soon after we left, he slipped into a coma.

I changed into my shorts, boots and mesh top, splashed cold water on my face and headed outside the restroom in Warm Springs, Montana. It didn't seem right to be backpacking while my father lay dying in the hospital. But, then again, nothing seemed right.

Greg returned from the men's restroom, and we put our jeans and t-shirts into a plastic bag. At the counter we asked if we could leave our clothes at the store while we hiked north. We would pick them up when we came back through in a month.

The owner was an older woman, slightly prone more toward scowls than smiles. "Just clothes, you say?" She leaned forward, peering into the bag.

"Yeah, see?" I said, pulling out the first few items. "We wore them on the bus ride but won't need them while we hike." I looked into her curious brown eyes.

A man taller than most moseyed up; he appeared to be a rancher. "Where you hiking?" he asked.

"Through Helena National Forest, then along the Continental Divide to Canada," Greg answered.

"Oh, oh, that's some hiking you'll be doing. Well, I'll tell you what, I'm the Deputy Sheriff here, and I'll just tell you one thing." He lifted his cowboy hat and straightened his hair. "You watch out up there."

"For bears?" I asked, trying to hurry him a little.

"Oh, yeah, for bears, but what I was going to tell you that you need to watch out for is mountain lions. There's lots of them."

Mountain lions! We'd been warned of rattlesnakes and grizzly bears, avalanches and river crossings, but no one had mentioned mountain lions!

"You keep an eye on your backs. They like to circle around behind you, and when you're not looking come right at you." He made a pouncing motion with his arms.

I jumped back.

"Oh, sorry, miss. I didn't mean to startle you. Just be careful out there."

"Thank you, Sheriff, we'll keep that in mind," Greg said.

I turned back to the owner, but she waved us off, "Don't worry about your clothes, they'll be here when you get back. Just take care of yourselves."

We thanked her and headed outside.

"Jesus Christ," Greg whispered as he adjusted his pack. "Do you think that's for real? They've got mountain lions attacking people out here?"

"I've heard of it before, but usually just solo hikers or kids." I flung my pack on. "But you know how people are, Greg, always wanting to scare us off the trail. We just can't let it get to us."

Nonetheless, that night, as I stepped from the tent and squatted to pee, I couldn't shake the feeling that a mountain lion was lurking in the tree line, waiting to come right at me. Wishing we'd never met that sheriff, I finished my business and hurried back into the tent.

Our next leg of the hike, from Warm Springs, Montana, north to the Canadian border would be our shortest but we hoped our most spectacular. In this 400-mile stretch we would hike through one of the largest wilderness areas in the United States, the Bob Marshall Wilderness Area, and visit Glacier National Park, renowned for the stunning beauty of its craggy peaks and aquamarine lakes.

It took us several days to get our trail-legs back. We felt sluggish and out of shape, frequently lost our route, and it rained — a lot. But on the night of July 2 we were camped on a hilltop that offered a 360-degree view of rolling hills and a startling sunset of yellow, orange and red clouds. I took several pictures, then lowered my camera and watched the sunset fade.

This is why they call it Big Sky Country, I thought, straining my neck to see it all. It didn't make sense to me that there could be more sky in Montana than in New York, but it was true. There was so much I couldn't take it all in without lying flat on my back, and, even then, I had to turn my head in every direction.

I peered into a steep gully and tried to picture Dana Spring at its bottom.

"What do you think, Jen, is this the way?" Greg asked.

It was early afternoon of the next day. We were low on water, and the spring we searched for was our only known source of water for ten miles. We needed to find it.

"Could be." I studied the map again. "Except there's supposed to be a road just beside the spring." I looked down the crowded gully. Trees rose from its steep banks, blocking our view of the far side and bottom. "I don't see a road here, and it seems a little steep for one, but maybe the map's wrong; it wouldn't be the first time."

The Helena National Forest map's inaccuracy with reference to Forest Service roads had been astounding, especially since the Forest Service published the map. Once beyond Warm Springs, we had suffered long hours of wasted effort before realizing we simply couldn't trust the map.

Well, I thought, we should be in Lincoln, Montana, by tomorrow and done with this lousy forest. But first we needed to find water. "Your GPS keeps pointing this way, right?" I wiped the sweat out of my eyes and looked at Greg. With the rains over and the temperature in the 80s, swarms of gnats and mosquitoes had come to life, and I swatted at them as I watched for Greg's reaction.

He nodded.

"If we figure the GPS is right and the map wrong, we might just find it down there," I said

Greg shrugged and put away his GPS. "May as well give it a try."

We both knew that saying the GPS was right was a bit misleading. It wasn't that it was malfunctioning, but in the interest of national security, the Department of Defense had once imposed Selective Availability (lifted in May 2000). This intentional degradation of the satellite signal resulted in all commercial GPS's having a built-in random error of up to one hundred meters. The closer we got to Dana Spring, the less accurate was our reading; and we were very close.

Pulling a branch from across his chest, Greg stepped over a log only to sink his foot into eight inches of vegetation. Buzzing gnats swarmed up from the undergrowth, sticking to his sweaty arms and neck. He slapped them away, and we continued hiking.

I followed close behind, holding onto thin saplings to maintain my balance on the steep slope. "This is going to be a bitch if we have to come back this way," I said, jinxing us. Sure enough, when we reached the bottom it was bone dry, and the GPS now pointed back up the gully. We mustered a surprising amount of patience and pulled ourselves back up the jinxed slope.

At the top we threw off our packs and flopped down. After resting, we circled back the way we came and discovered an old jeep road, the same one we crossed hours earlier. We followed it, emerging from the woods in front of the unmistakable wooden fence surrounding Dana Spring.

Unable to find water north of Black Mountain, Montana, we were forced to hike for eighteen hours before camping. (Photo: Greg Allen)

After lunch we ascended Black Mountain and followed the open ridgeline all afternoon. The view of the surrounding hillsides was striking, and though steep in places, the trail was clear and easily followed.

It was just getting dark when we reached the hill with the next spring. After searching in vain for twenty minutes, we decided to keep going and try our luck elsewhere. As it turned out, our luck wasn't too good that day. An hour later it was 10:00 p.m., and we were still hiking.

"Greg, can we take a break? My feet are killing me."

While in Indiana, a podiatrist had x-rayed both my feet for stress fractures. Finding none, he concluded the bones and ligaments were deeply bruised and had issued me a triple-strength anti-inflammatory. I took one of his little white pills and a baby-blue Aleve at breakfast and lunch every day. Even so, as I lay on my pack in the dark with my aching feet in the air, I felt I couldn't possibly endure the pain of putting on my boots and walking.

"Can we camp here tonight, Greg, and find water in the morning?"

"I'm sorry, Babe, I got to keep going. I am so thirsty and dehydrated; I can't imagine going to sleep without water."

I didn't cry. I just lay there rubbing the pads of my feet. Finally, I sighed, reached over my head into the hood of my pack and found my bag of ibuprofen.

We set out again. Soon it was too dark to make out even the roughest outline of our trail. Greg put on our only headlamp, and we walked side by side on the jeep road, dependant on the five-foot circle of light that emanated from Greg's forehead. Like a poorly rehearsed team in a potato sack race, we stumbled along that dark road for what felt like hours. Finally, I saw what I had been praying for.

"*Aqua,*" I said, using the Latin word for water.

"Where?"

I pointed beside the trail at a mound two feet high and eight feet

across. It was covered with gravel and pine needles, but beneath that
was the unmistakable glow of snow. Water. It took us nearly two hours
to melt it, cook dinner and lay out our sleeping bags.

"Can you set your alarm, Greg?"

"Sure, what time?"

"Five-thirty."

"Are you kidding? That's only three hours away."

"Well, I'm not positive, but I think we're about two or three miles
from the road that cuts into Lincoln, and it's twelve miles long. That
means we probably have fifteen miles to do tomorrow." Turning over
to try and get comfortable, I added, "And tomorrow is Saturday of the
Fourth of July weekend, remember? I checked our schedule; the Lincoln
Post Office closes at noon on Saturdays. So, I figured if we got up at
five-thirty and left by six, we would get there in time."

Sighing, he set his watch.

As tired as we were, our hips, legs and feet were in such pain from
being dehydrated that it was difficult to sleep. Thus ended what we
came to refer to as Dana Spring Day, eighteen hours of continuous
hiking.

After a sluggish start in the morning, we picked our way through a
clear-cut, crossed a stream and emerged on the gravel road to Lincoln.
Though we maintained our pace, after several hours we grew concerned
about reaching the Post Office too late.

We hiked faster, the drill being:

*Hike for sixty minutes, rest for seven, just enough time to
sit on my pack, take off boots and socks, rub left foot, right
foot, left foot, right foot, put socks back on, ease boots
back on, stand up, pee, put on pack.*

Either the road was longer than we thought or we were moving more slowly. We weren't going to make it. Around ten o'clock a silver pick-up with a dented white cab stopped beside us.

"Where you two headed?" the driver asked. He was an older gentleman with curly brown hair and a dimpled smile. His wife leaned forward to watch.

"Lincoln," we answered in unison.

John and Faye Graves had driven out from their home in Great Falls, Montana, that morning and were passing through Lincoln as part of a four-day weekend away. An ex-Marine, John was delighted to hear we planned to hike all the way to Canada.

"I suppose you won't accept a ride into Lincoln, will you?" John asked.

We declined the ride. "But could you stop by the Post Office and drop off a note?" I asked. Finding paper, I wrote to the Postmistress explaining that we might arrive ten or fifteen minutes past noon and please stay open until we arrived. The Graves took the note and drove off. I felt like I had put a message in a bottle and tossed it into the ocean.

An hour later we saw the familiar silver pick-up. Faye rolled down her window and handed us a note. "From the Postmistress," she explained.

Written in pencil on the torn bottom of a sheet of paper was "Jennifer, I have your packages. I'll try to stay open, but if we're closed when you get here, call me at home." A phone number was written on the bottom and beneath that, "Mary Barrish, Lincoln Postmistress." I looked away, once again moved to tears by the kindness of strangers. After months of battling the uncaring wilderness, human contact had never seemed so precious.

Having given our thanks to the Graves, we waved goodbye and continued our march into Lincoln, a little more slowly and a lot more relaxed. We reached the Post Office at twelve-thirty. It was closed. As we were discussing where to find a pay phone, Mary drove by and re-opened for us. The day was saved, or so it seemed.

After checking into our room at the local motel, I called my mother's house. My sister, Kathy Keirsey, answered the phone and told me that Dad was deep in his coma, his breathing labored and forced. His oncologist had said, "It's time for the hikers to come home."

We flew home to Indiana and arrived in time to see Dad once more before he died. Then, on the morning of July 10, he quietly slipped away.

The funeral followed a few days later, hundreds of thank you cards were written and sent, most of the family dispersed and there was nothing left for us to do. My youngest sister, Amy, was planning to stay with Mom for the duration of the summer, so Greg and I returned to Montana.

As we flew west I stared out the window and marveled that life could go on with my dad no longer alive. It seemed outrageous that this could happen. I wanted to stop total strangers and shake them, screaming, "How can this be?" But I didn't. I sat quietly and allowed the minutes to pile one on top of the other, leaving my father behind.

He had accomplished a great deal during his sixty-seven years, but while staring blankly at the seats in front of me, I recalled the one dream he had never realized. My father had always wanted to become a sea captain, sailing around the world for glory and treasure. To this day I don't know if he was serious or just made it up to entertain his children; but it struck my fancy, and I often thought of it.

At times it seemed sad that he never fulfilled his dream, while at other times, like now, it steeled my determination to pursue my own goals. Though I was depressed and apathetic in the aftermath of my father's funeral, I was adamant about finishing the Continental Divide Trail. My father could no longer achieve his dream, but I could and would.

Our route through the Helena National Forest continued to be obscure, and two days north of Lincoln it disappeared entirely. Fifty acres of felled trees, stumps and stripped branches were partially concealed by tall grass. It was a clear-cut. With surprising grace for his size, Greg wove his way across the littered field. I followed. Nervous about twisting an ankle or gouging an eye, I picked my way over and around the worst of the obstacles. Meanwhile, grasshoppers clickity-clacked all around as they leaped in the tall grass. One ricocheted off my sunglasses, reminding me to keep my mouth firmly shut.

Forty-five minutes later we came to the end of the clear-cut. The trail was nowhere in sight. We split up to look for it, knowing that if we could find it in fifteen to twenty minutes, it would be time well spent. The alternative, bushwhacking, was sure to be frustrating and slow. We never found it.

"This is crazy," I said angrily, when we regrouped to find a new route. "It's bad enough they annihilated this forest and destroyed this wild habitat with their brutal clear-cut. But the least they could do is require the loggers to re-establish the trail they destroyed. Even if they don't rebuild it, couldn't they have flagged it to indicate where we could pick it up on the edges of the clear-cut?"

Greg nodded but didn't respond. Gazing at the display on the GPS, he backed from the trees in an effort to link with a satellite. Or maybe he was just trying to get away from my grumpiness.

"How many satellites you got?" I demanded.

"Two."

"At least they could update their maps once in a while. Not like this clear-cut hasn't been here for ten years." Falling silent, I tapped the tip of my trekking pole against the toe of my boot and noticed that the thick leather was beginning to crack.

"Bingo!" he said. "Ready?"

He rattled off the latitude and longitude, and I located our position on the map. Then I gave him the coordinates of the closest water source along our route. He entered this into the GPS and waited for it to compute our distance and direction to the spring. I used my compass and map to do the same, a drill we had performed hundreds of times.

"Five point one miles, three hundred and five degrees," he said.

"Sounds good," I confirmed. "I've got three hundred."

After putting away the map and GPS, I held out the compass. "Want to go first?" I asked.

"Sure."

He reached past the compass, took hold of my outstretched wrist and gently pulled me toward him.

"Honey, I'm sorry I got mad," I said, leaning into him. "It's just so frustrating at times."

"Don't worry about it, Jen, it's all right." Poles dangling from both wrists, he held me in his arms and kissed me.

Resting my head against his chest, I closed my eyes and wished it all away: the clear-cut, my aching feet, the smell of sun-block and insect repellant, my father's death. Greg stroked my arms, and I listened to the grasshoppers. Tears filled my eyes, and I held him tight.

After several deep breaths, I gave him another kiss and said, "Honey, how's your foot doing?"

He was thoughtful. "It's not as bad as before, but it still hurts. I think the cortisone shot I had in Denver is helping, but I have to be careful with it. If I step on a rock, especially if I hit it at an angle, it hurts a lot."

I didn't know what to say, so I gave him a tight smile and kissed him on each cheek.

That night, I woke with a start . . . "Dad," I mumbled. A dream floated back to me.

My father, alive and healthy, was seated in a cafe across from my sister, Carnie. They had met for lunch at the Indianapolis Circle and were laughing together as they ate their salads on the terrace. The sun rippled through the tall buildings as the breeze ruffled the napkins on their table.

In the pitch dark I rolled on my back and wriggled my arms up through the sleeping bag. I pressed the Indiglo — three-thirty in the morning. I listened to the night sounds: Greg's soft snore, a slight breeze, no rain.

I closed my eyes and again saw my father. He leaned forward and said something to my sister. I strained to hear what was passed between them. His gold-capped tooth flashed and his body shook as he laughed at the joke he had told.

My chest tightened.

Oh, Dad, why did you have to die?

Hiking past the Chinese Wall in the Bob Marshall Wilderness Area, Montana. (Photo: Greg Allen)

On July 24, a week later, we hiked into East Glacier, Montana, and stopped by its Post Office. I sat next to our packs and waited outside while Greg retrieved our mail. He brought out the largest packages first: our supply box, snowshoes and miscellaneous items we forwarded from Lincoln. I glanced at our growing pile of gear and closed my eyes to enjoy the tingle of my unburdened feet. Leaning my head against the brick wall of the government building, I felt the warmth of the sun on my up-turned face and could distantly hear someone climb out of their car and slam the door.

After some time I became aware that Greg stood over me. Squinting up at him, I looked past the letter he was reading and spied the small box tucked under his arm.

I sat up and fished out my knife. "Here, give me that box."

Without a word, he handed me the package and sat down beside me.

Swiftly cutting through the tape and paper, I opened the box and dug out a handful of homemade, chocolate-chip cookies. Dumping those in Greg's lap, I pulled out several for myself and began reading the enclosed letter from my friend, Pat DeToffel.

Half a box of cookies and two letters later, Greg opened the envelope from the Glacier National Park Service and studied the enclosed permit. "Jen, this is nothing like we requested."

"Let me see." I dropped my letter as I leaned over Greg's shoulder to read the permit. "I have to check the maps, but off the top of my head their route doesn't put us anywhere near the Continental Divide!"

"Listen to the daily mileage, Jen, eleven point three, thirteen, twelve point five." Greg smiled. "Guess they didn't believe us when we said we wanted to hike eighteen to twenty miles per day. Looks like we're going to have one easy week of hiking."

I was angry and disappointed to be leaving the trail once again. I had often fantasized about snowshoeing over Ahern Drift and hiking on the narrow ledge of the Highline Trail. Instead we were being routed through the lower elevations east of the Divide. I suspected there was still snow on the higher trails and they wanted to keep people's boots from destroying the fragile alpine growth.

That afternoon Greg called their backcountry office to see if we could get through Glacier in four days instead of five. No go. The campsites were fully booked. By then I had grown used to the idea, and I didn't mind too much; it would be a nice break. But I was concerned about the lost time. We were going to have to hurry to finish by October 6, our projected end date. Of course, we didn't know when it would start snowing in the fall; but, as the summer progressed, I became convinced that we needed to get out of the Rockies by the first week in October. As it turned out, my prediction was right. The southern San Juan Mountains received their first winter snowstorm on October 8, heavy enough to shut down the road through Wolf Creek Pass.

Lingering in town the next morning, we bought ice cream cones, a t-shirt for Greg and a birthday present for my mom. We needed to have our permits stamped in Two Medicine Campground by four in the afternoon, but it was only twelve miles away, and the lure of being a tourist was strong. As such, we were late getting started, and as we labored to the trail's high point of 7,522 feet with full packs, we realized we had underestimated these twelve miles.

From the top we had four miles to go and an hour to get there. Propelling ourselves down the mountain as quickly as we could, we jogged and limped on the straight stretches while clutching our pouches to our sides. Other hikers gave us wide berth as we shuffled past them, red faced and sweating.

Coming into the campground with eight minutes to spare, we laughed at our foolishness in cutting it so close. We didn't care. We were having fun. It was only 4:00 p.m., and we had the rest of the day to enjoy the campground's hot showers, flush toilets, picnic tables and convenience store. While everyone around us was roughing it, we were living it up.

Over the next two days we leisurely made our way north through
the beautiful Glacier National Park. Though the mosquitoes were
horrendous, and the trails were sometimes overgrown, the slower pace
and easy route was a balm to my grieving spirit. I had plenty of time to
cry as I walked and didn't have to give anything much effort. Even
during the times I was engrossed in my chores or laboring up a steep
climb, the hike drew me out of my head and my memories, gently
forcing me to attend to today. As much as I hated to admit it, life was
moving on without my father and taking me with it.

Low-mileage days and stunning vistas made hiking through Glacier National
Park, Montana a highlight of the summer. (Photo: Greg Allen)

We camped at the base of Triple Divide Mountain and then continued north to Piegan Pass. The morning was gray and blustery, threatening rain. As we climbed on a narrow ledge, the wind howled overhead, while the straps on my pack snapped loudly, occasionally striking my neck and face. The pass flattened into a rocky saddle between two peaks. To our left dark cliffs towered hundreds of feet into the air, dwarfing us like some ancient fortress. Somewhere on the top of that ridge lay the Highline Trail I had so badly wanted to hike. Seeing what I would have faced, I didn't mind missing Highline so much.

We climbed the last hundred yards and were hit with fifty-mile-per-hour winds. Our pants and jackets were plastered against our bodies as we fought for balance in the tumultuous conditions.

I had taken several steps across the open pass when a sudden gust lifted me completely off my feet, dropping me to the ground a foot away. Shaken, I rose to a low crouch, spread my legs wide and continued. My trekking poles scraped uselessly against the bare rock as I fought for purchase.

As we descended the north face of the pass, the wind dropped off, and with it came moments of relative calm amid the sudden gusts.

"This is cool!" Greg shouted during a lull.

I smiled in return. This was definitely exciting. Just then, a burst of wind caught us off guard, and we dropped to the ground.

Greg pointed to the cliff top and made a spooky Halloween face. Laughing, we rose again, ready for the wind's challenge.

Leading the way, Greg began his awkward shuffle. Like a turtle trying to walk on its two hind legs, he balanced his heavy pack as he walked with bent knees and outstretched arms. A gust slammed into his side, throwing his weight onto his injured left foot. He cried out, dropping to one knee.

I ached to help him, but I couldn't think of a thing to do. After resting a minute, he carefully tested his left foot, easing more weight onto it as he rose on both feet. When we reached a clump of low bushes shielded by a room-sized boulder we stopped and took off our packs. Greg removed his boot and held his left thigh in the air, twisting his ankle from side to side. He reached forward and squeezed the pad of his foot with both hands. At long last he admitted, "It hurts, Jen."

I saw the worry in his hazel eyes as he leaned against his pack, his injured limb resting on his right knee.

"When I land on it wrong, streaks of pain shoot as far as my knee." His words were filled with despair. "And all it takes is a little stone to twist my foot to its side. Jen, there are stones everywhere. I can't see them all . . ."

I waited in silence for him to continue, but he didn't. "Do you want another ibu?" I asked. He nodded. I gave him two ibuprofens from the Ziploc in my pouch.

Water bottle in hand, he stared at the swirling clouds on top of the cliff. "Actually," he said, "I can live with the pain. It's not as bad as it was in the past. But I'm worried about making it worse. How much longer before it becomes permanent?" Neither of us ventured a guess. "I really don't want an operation. Who knows what'll happen after they cut out the nerve? The doctor said that some people never regain any feeling in their foot at all. Jen, what if that happened to me? Would I be able to run, hike, ski?"

"Maybe it won't get that bad," I said, trying to reassure him. "It always feels better when you get into town and are off it for a couple of days."

"Maybe."

"Why don't we try another cortisone shot after we get out of Glacier? If it works, then I bet you won't be damaging the nerve more."

"Yeah, you might be right," he said as he pulled his boot back on. "But I've got to tell you, Babe, this sucks. All I want is to be able to continue hiking without it hurting like this. Is that too much to ask?"

I squeezed his forearm, saying, "Greg, what is it you're always telling me . . . that everything's going to be all right? God has a plan, remember?" He didn't shrug me away. "And God doesn't make mistakes. I don't know what will happen with your foot, but I trust God's will. He loves you perfectly and is powerful enough to make anything happen. It's not an accident that your foot is acting up. There must be a reason. We just don't know what it is."

Greg's injured foot continuously worsened on the rocky trails of Glacier National Park. (Photo: Jennifer Hanson)

Nodding slowly, he kissed me on the forehead, and we held each other for a long, long time.

As we continued hiking I began to think that Greg might not be able to finish. I didn't know what lengths he would go to stay on the trail, but I knew he would not give up easily. My thoughts drifted back to a night during our first winter together. Greg wanted to get his father's old snowmobile working and take me for a ride. It must have been close to midnight and zero degrees as he bent over that machine in his father's unheated shed.

I held the flashlight as he tinkered with the engine, cleaned the spark plugs and pulled again and again on that frayed rip-chord. Surely he'll give up soon and we can go to bed, I kept thinking. But he never did. For over an hour he labored on that ghost of a snowmobile. Finally, it coughed itself awake, and we had our moon-lit ride. I really didn't know what it would take for Greg to leave the trail, but I knew it would have to be very bad.

I moved on as the trail dropped steadily into the lush valley. Thick undergrowth crowded out the path while mosquitoes hovered everywhere, even to the point of viciously biting through the fabric of my long-sleeved shirt. Swatting continuously, I thought more about our situation.

Just as Greg may have no choice but to stop, I didn't feel I had much choice but to continue. (After the summer ended I was surprised when people asked about my decision to continue hiking after Greg left. As disappointed as I was for him, it never even occurred to me to leave the trail myself.)

I was thoroughly enjoying hiking on the CDT, despite its trials and tribulations. Even with all the discomfort involved, it was worth it to me. On the trail I was blessed with a life of simple pleasures, stiff challenges, gorgeous vistas and frequent encounters with wildlife. In contrast, there was little besides Greg waiting for me in New York: no job, no home and no family.

Unlike my husband, who had a very good reason to stop, I didn't. Or at least I didn't think so at the time. It wasn't something my mother raised me to see as an option. As a seven-year-old child, I had been allowed to join my sisters' swim team; I walked a mile each morning to practice in a cold, outdoor pool littered with leaves and bugs. Though I woke with a stomachache nearly every day and was scared at the thought of brushing against a big, black beetle, I learned not to ask if I could skip practice.

"You can go back to bed," Mom always reminded me, "but if you skip practice, you have to quit the team."

I enjoyed the competition and challenge too much to quit, and for the next fourteen years, I never missed a practice, game or class without a very good reason. Perhaps this is part of why it never occurred to me *not* to finish the CDT.

I came to an area of uprooted and trampled weeds. Grizzly bear, I realized; they dug up these plants in search of grubs. The freshly exposed earth was a moist, dark brown while the edges were a paler tan. Been drying for about an hour, I guessed. I looked around slowly, smelled the air and listened, trying to discern which way the bear went. I searched the trail for tracks, but the ground was too well packed for my inexperienced eye. The grizzly could be anywhere.

"Yoa, bear," I called out. We had read that the human voice was the most effective bear deterrent. Unless they were accustomed to getting food from humans, most animals would do what they could to avoid contact with people. The trick was to be heard before you were seen. "Yoa, bear!" I bellowed into the valley.

I knew Greg would hear me and be more cautious. Not waiting for him to catch up, I continued across the meadow. At its far edge the trail wound through a dense growth of pine and shrub. I couldn't see farther than ten feet down the winding path. Imagining a grizzly just out of view, a chill raced down my spine, and I slowed my pace. "Yoa, bear!" I hollered again. And suddenly I wondered how I would deal with bears if Greg dropped out.

My throat tightened at the thought of a bear attack, but as I continued down the trail, I reviewed the precautions I would take to prevent an encounter in the first place: watch for bear signs and habitat, call out loudly and hang my food far from camp. In all our months on the trail, Greg had always hung our food bags. It was a tedious, sometimes difficult chore of selecting an appropriate tree branch, slinging the rope over the top and pulling up the food bags. Sound simple? It wasn't. Good branches were sometimes hard to find, our rope could become stuck in the tree, and it wasn't uncommon to set up camp in the dark. I'll just have to do the best I can, I thought, and learn the hard way — like Greg did.

As a last defense against bear attack, I carried a five-inch tube of Capisene pepper spray. Supposedly, it would cause a bear to flee if I sprayed into its face. It wasn't easy to feel protected by such a tiny device, considering that the bear had to be within ten feet for it to be effective, but it was all I had. Besides, I wouldn't soon forget how it felt the time I accidentally sprayed myself. Within seconds I was choking and spitting, tears pouring down my face. An hour later, my lips were still numb. Others had told me it worked as well as mace, which made me think of men. Anxiety rippled through me again.

For the most part I would be alone in the mountains. I wasn't concerned about the handful of ranchers, loggers or forest service personnel I was likely to run across. Likewise, I generally felt safe in town. It was the in-between zone that made me nervous. The foothills were often covered with dirt roads that might lead to favorite drinking spots for a truck-load of guys on a Friday night.

Still, I had hiked alone enough to know what to do. It wasn't fun hiding in the bushes each time I heard someone coming or spying on a group of campers to decide if it was safe to walk past them. But it had worked before, and it would work again.

Whatever happens, I thought, I have my pepper spray!

Brandishing the tiny can like a sword, I silently proclaimed that it would work just like mace — on man or beast or beastly men.

"Yoa, bear!" I hurled down the trail. It occurred to me there could be aspects of hiking alone that I might enjoy. I would no longer have to make the inevitable compromises that came from hiking with another person. I wouldn't have to filter water, a weary chore. I would carry iodine tablets and mail the filter home. Better yet, I would never have to eat ramen again. I tried to imagine being alone for three or four days on end. I could stop when I wanted, hike where I chose, pray and meditate without interruption. I took a deep, easy breath, relaxing more fully than I had all morning. Quickening my pace, I imagined moving swiftly through the mountains, navigating through the forests, relying on no one but myself, dropping into town for a well-deserved break.

"I am woman, hear me roar, in numbers too big to ignore," I sang. It had been over twenty years since I was in high school, lying on the floor of my girlfriend's room, bellowing out Helen Reddy's tune; but it felt just as good now as it had then.

I finished what I could remember of the song and looked back to find Greg. He was nowhere in sight. Feeling guilty, I sat down to wait. I wondered what it might be like for him — if he had to quit. I knew in some ways he would be glad to get home. He had a twenty-foot bass boat, two dogs, a good job, and his family and friends to welcome him back. But I couldn't imagine how hard it would be for him to come so far and not be able to finish.

After several minutes he appeared at the far end of the trail, moving slowly through the dense undergrowth. I watched as he slapped a mosquito off his shoulder, and the familiar sweep of his arm was suddenly precious to me.

My God, I thought, I'm going to miss him! I wrapped my arms tightly around myself in consolation. Doubt raced through me. I wondered what I would do if he was no longer there to make me laugh. How would I ever keep going without his boots luring me up a long climb? Who would coax me over a stream or cheer me with hot chocolate? And when I stood at the top of a mountain and wanted to tell someone how incredibly gorgeous the view was and how lucky I was to be alive, no one would be there to hear me.

Once we reached Canada we asked the border guard on Chief Joseph Highway to take our picture then caught a ride back to East Glacier on a tour bus. It was pleasantly odd to drive swiftly past the mountains we had just spent five days sweating over — seated on a tour bus, eating ice cream and listening to the driver's playful chatter.

In Kalispell a podiatrist gave Greg yet another cortisone shot. He claimed to be an expert on Morton's neuroma since he suffered from it as well. He gave Greg a shot of his most powerful concoction, saying, "If this doesn't work, nothing will."

From our motel room, I called home.

"Hanson's, Lois speaking," my mother said. Dad had insisted on this phone greeting. It wouldn't do for a Colonel's family to be picking up the phone saying a plain old, "Hello."

I briefly shared with my mother the story of our week and asked how she was doing.

"Oh, fine, fine. Amy and I have been keeping busy fixing up the house, doing what we can for the garden. It's been so neglected this year with all that's happened."

All that's happened, I thought. How could her loss be so neatly wrapped in those three words? "It's been pretty quiet, eh?"

"Oh, no. I've had more visitors than ever, the Garsts and Millers, Mr. McKeeman from the office, the women from the church. And, of course, one of the men from the VFW is over just about every day. Everyone wants to be helpful, but, really, there's so little they can do." Her voice trailed off, and I felt a lump in my throat. "Did I tell you Amy and I are going to drive up to Rice Lake?" she ended brightly.

"Yeah, Mom, you said that in your letter. That sounds great."

It had been over a year since she had visited her mother in Wisconsin; the twelve-hour drive was too much for Dad. Not wanting to make the trip alone, she squeezed it in before Amy had to return to college.

"So, Mom, how *are* you doing?" I heard her take a deep breath.

"I'm doing okay, dear. I have my good days and my bad, but it's been three weeks now. Hard to believe."

I agreed. It seemed impossible that three whole weeks had passed. At times I still struggled with the feeling that the world should have stopped spinning the moment Dad died.

Fourth Leg

From Warm Springs, MT south to South Pass, WY

Chapter 8

Greg's Goodbye
Warm Springs, MT south to Wisdom, MT

Greg and I entered the Anaconda-Pintlar Wilderness through its northern border two days later. It was August 5, and we had begun the fourth leg of our hike: Warm Springs, Montana to South Pass, Wyoming. Over the next five weeks we would be hiking through the Anaconda-Pintlar, Bitterroot Range, Yellowstone National Park and the Wind River Range. These were high altitude mountains blocked by snow earlier in the summer.

I plunged down the well-groomed trail, glancing briefly to find Greg not far behind. Stepping carefully to avoid twisting his foot, he was totally consumed with the task of avoiding further pain and injury. I slowed, matching my pace with his.

"Jen, have you thought of what you will do if I have to drop out?" It was as if Greg had been reading my mind. "A little," I ventured.

"You'd go on alone, wouldn't you?" His eyebrows were knit in concentration as he studied the roots that traversed our trail. Winding his way around the tree trunk, he glanced at me, his calmness reassuring.

"Yeah, I would like to continue and finish if I can." Grateful to finally talk about it, I hurried on, adding, "I've been trying to think of ways to cut back on weight."

"Yeah, you'd have to do that. You can't possibly take the stuff I've been carrying: the tent, water filter, stove and fuel. Your pack would be well over forty pounds, and that would be murder in these mountains."

"Well, I've been thinking of a bivy sack. It'd suck not having a tent any longer, but at least a bivy sack would keep my bag dry and mosquitoes out of my face. Also, I could purify my water with iodine tablets and send the water filter home. That would save me three or four pounds."

"Oooh, iodine," he teased and made a yucky face.

"Oh, it doesn't taste that bad. I'm used to it." I waited while he maneuvered through a particularly rocky area and asked, "So, what about you, hon? What would you do back home?"

"Well, it would be nice to take some time off, get the boat out, see the dogs." He smiled. "But I suppose I should go back to work. We could use the money."

When he reached me I kissed him. "I love you, Greg."

He smiled warmly and kissed me back. "I love you too. Now get going, or we'll never get there before dark."

A day later we crossed over Rainbow Saddle and posed for snapshots at its battered sign. Daisies, lupine and Indian paintbrush had filled the pass; they lined our trail as it wound up and over the rocky slopes.

At dusk we reached Warren Lake, surrounded by a narrow band of spruce trees and circled by red, white and gray cliffs. I stood at the water's edge before filling my pot, watching fish rise to the surface in search of bugs. Unseen frogs croaked and the faintest of breezes rippled the surface of the lake. I found myself thinking of my father, as I did so often these days. I heard myself whispering:

"If I have to go on alone, you'll watch over me, won't you, Dad?"

Since he was no longer confined to a shriveled body in Indiana, he seemed closer now, as though he might be all around me: strong, loving and attentive. I didn't want to hold him back from his spiritual journey, but I also felt he wanted to be with me on the hike.

Just before midnight we were awakened by a shuffling sound outside our tent. Peering through the vestibule with our flashlight, we spotted two mule deer pawing the ground where we had urinated earlier. They seemed undisturbed by our light and were still grazing a dozen feet away when we fell back to sleep.

The next afternoon we topped the final ridgeline in the southern section of the Wilderness Area. With a commanding view of the valley east of the mountains and the Bitterroot Range in the south, we stopped to rest. I propped my pack against my hiking pole, creating a backrest from which I could gaze south along the open ridge. The Bitterroot Range was snowcapped and jagged, and I felt a wave of trepidation as I studied them for the first time.

I recalled my father's stories of these mountains that spanned the border of Montana and Idaho. At the age of eighteen, he and his brother, Tom, had spent a summer working for the forest rangers in the Bitterroot Range. The high peaks, clear mountain lakes and thick underbrush had left a deep impression on Dad. He had advised me to wear tough pants, for they were sure to be ripped to shreds by the undergrowth. I looked down at my running shorts, hoping that, for once, he was wrong. Then Greg's next comment put a screeching halt to my dad's advice.

"Jen, I'm going to stop."

I turned to search his face.

He was staring at a stick he held in his hands, tapping it repeatedly against his thigh. "I'm holding you up and probably damaging the nerve further." He grimaced. "God, I want to finish the hike!" He threw down the stick and looked away. "You don't know how often I've dreamt of us hiking into Chama, finishing the trail together." A tear spilled onto his cheek.

Aching for him, I went to Greg and wrapped my arms around him. There was no arguing or holding out hope this time. He had been limping severely the past few days.

"But I can't, I just can't," he moaned. "It hurts so damn bad, Jen. And when it isn't hurting like hell, then I'm afraid I'm going to step on it wrong, and it will hurt. That's what really sucks, Jen, never knowing what the next step will bring."

I rubbed his arms in a futile attempt to comfort him. He took a deep breath, and now it was my turn to step away and give him room.

"But listen, Jen, I want you to keep going. I want you to go all the way. Do it for the both of us. God, I'm already jealous of you." He paused, as if to collect his thoughts and be able to say all the right words to me. Finally: "I wish like hell I could finish, but I want you to know I'll totally support *your* hike."

I managed a thank you that didn't do justice to the moment. Then I realized it was really happening. Now it was up to me. A rush of feelings swept through me: grief, fear, guilt, excitement.

Greg took another deep breath and rubbed his face with his hands. Staring across the hilltop into the ranch dotted eastern horizon, he seemed calmer and more peaceful than he had in weeks. Swinging his gaze farther south, he asked, "Did you see the Bitterroots? They look vicious."

"Yeah, I'm trying not to look at them. They scare me."

"Ah, you'll be fine. Mountains always look worse from far away."

We drifted into silence, each absorbed in our own thoughts.

After a while, Greg said, "First thing I'll do when I get home is get my boat out. Take the dogs fishing."

With that statement he seemed twenty feet away instead of two. I felt a sudden pain in my body and tried to breath past it. He must have felt it too; he stopped talking about home.

Instead, he said, "Well, I guess if we want to be in Wisdom by tomorrow, we better get going."

Not ready to go, I hugged him. He wrapped me in his arms. My tears came in a rush, and it felt like the days following our miscarriage. Days in which we moved wildly between grief, anger, shame and, oddly, joy.

Through the rest of the day, we stopped often, our schedule no longer important. We hugged or cried, talked about his going home, people's reactions, my hiking alone. A day later we went through our "last times." Last time we had lunch together; last time he filtered water; last time we set up our tent. We decided to make our last night special by building a fire, something we had never done before.

Greg went into the trees in search of wood. In a few minutes he returned, shaking his head in disbelief, arms filled with cut logs. In this empty, empty forest so far from anything and at the exact place we decided to camp, someone had cut and stacked a cord of wood!

The following day, August 10, we reached Highway 43 and hitched a ride into Wisdom, Montana. After dropping our packs and mail in our motel room, Greg went in search of a phone. Instead of following my normal routine of preparing our food and maps for the next section, I left our supply box on the bed, unopened.

I stuffed our clothes in my sleeping bag pouch and walked across the street to a coin laundry. By the time I got back, Greg had returned. His hair was still wet from a shower, and he was reading his mail.

"How did the calls go?" I tried.

"Mom was great," he said. "She was telling me how much the dogs are missing me and how excited she was to have me coming home." His face flushed. "She even made me promise to take her out in the boat."

I got up and sat next to Greg, smoothing the hair from his temple. "She's a good Mom you got, Greg, definitely a keeper." (A "keeper" is a fish that's big enough to qualify in a bass tournament.)

He smiled at the reference.

"Did you tell Luke? He'll need to know to send less food in the supply packages." I stumbled over the last words, unable to say "my" supply packages.

"Not yet." He dropped his mail on the bed. "I'm not ready yet, Jen. I know Luke will be super supportive, but . . ." He shrugged.

"No biggie, Greg. He's probably already sent the next couple of packages anyway. Another few days won't make much difference."

The morning after that conversation I walked down the street and opened the screen door to the general store. The wooden floor creaked as I slowly moved down the cluttered aisle and waited for my eyes to adjust to the dark. They had everything here: clothes, groceries, sporting goods, stationery and more. I picked up a lightweight, collapsible blade to replace my bulky Swiss Army knife, a tool I rarely used anyway. In addition, I replaced our headlamp with a plastic flashlight the size of a single AA battery.

Greg found me in the back, thumbing through the used paperbacks. "Find anything you like?" he asked.

"Hey, what are you doing up?" I looked down at his foot, as if I expected it to answer me. "How does it feel?"

"Oh, you know, it always feels better in town where there are no rocks or roots."

I put down the book and pulled him close to me. "Well, that's good. Probably means there's no permanent damage."

"I know, but I just wish it would give me a shooting pain every once in a while and tell me I've made the right decision."

Normally I would say something encouraging — but not now. He would have to live with this decision for the rest of his life, and it had to be his decision, not mine.*

"Anyway, how's the shopping?" he asked.

I showed him what I'd picked out. "But I haven't found any lightweight rope. Did you see any?"

He went in search of lightweight rope and returned with two hundred feet of parachute chord. It fit in the palm of my hand and weighed three ounces. I remembered the professional climbing rope

---

* As it turned out, Greg did end up needing foot surgery to remove his injured nerve. It was completely successful and eliminated all of the pain while retaining full functioning of his foot.

we carried at the beginning of the hike. It was special ordered, indestructible, bulky — and heavy as hell.

We headed back to the motel and spread the gear on our bed. Greg leaned against the headboard as I began sorting my food into neat piles of breakfast, lunch, dinner and snacks. "Want to help?"

He nodded.

I handed him our bag of spices, and he dumped half of each into the wastebasket. The room filled with the aroma of curry powder, cinnamon and black pepper. He started sneezing, and I laughed, then sneezed myself.

When we finished I looked at the small piles of rice, beans, pasta and cereal. It was probably enough for five days, but I sure wasn't going to be "fat and happy" when I got to Leadore, Idaho. I finished loading my pack and slipped it on to gauge its weight.

"Doable." I sighed. "Probably thirty-two pounds. Two more for the bivy sack makes it thirty-four." I was disappointed that it was still so heavy, but I couldn't think of what else to discard.

I remembered what my father said about pack weight. It was during a conversation last February when he was assessing my preparedness without appearing to do so. He asked how heavy my pack was. I told him I hoped to keep it at less than thirty-two pounds, which would be the equivalent of an average man carrying forty-four. He nodded agreement, explaining that as an Army infantry officer, he was adamant that his men not carry more than forty-two pounds. If heavier, many would not be able to sustain a twenty-mile forced march.

I turned to Greg, almost pleading, "Do you think this is crazy? Do you really think I can do it?"

He hopped off the bed and stood before me. "Absolutely, Babe. I know you can do this. You have everything it takes. You're an excellent navigator, strong hiker, incredibly determined — and you have tons of courage. Hell, I feel more confident in you going alone than I would about myself."

That might be true, but I was scared. What if we were wrong? What if I couldn't cut it? Though my stomach tightened at the thought, I ignored it. I would not go home without trying.

Now there was only one thing left to do — I needed to tell my mom. I had wanted to wait until I thought I could do it without crying, but I ran out of time.

Greg went off to the café to order dinner, while I crossed the street to use the pay phone at the gas station. Evening traffic rumbled down Main Street as I pressed the receiver to one ear, my thumb to the other.

"That's right, Mom, he's decided to stop hiking and return to New York. He's going back to work." I paused, waiting for the question I didn't want to answer. But she was silent. I filled the void with, "It's probably best, you know. So he doesn't damage it permanently."

Even then she didn't ask.

"So, he's catching a ride to the bus station tonight," I said. "A guy is coming down from Butte to bring me a bivy sack, and he's agreed to give Greg a lift. He'll take a bus to Lander, where our car is waiting, and be back in New York —"

"And you?" she interrupted, her voice rising. "You're not thinking of going on, are you?"

"Well, yeah, Mom, I'm going to finish. I'll be fine," I rushed to assure her. "I'll be real careful. I know what I'm doing, Mom, really. And there's a ranger station here in Wisdom. I spoke to them this afternoon about my route."

I wasn't asking for her permission exactly. I had been on my own too long for that. Yet I felt guilty. I didn't want to give her more to worry about after all she had been through. I suppose I called expecting her sympathy, and perhaps awed concern, for it had not occurred to me that she might actually object. She never had before, but then again I had never set out to hike alone through 900 miles of the Rocky Mountains.

The phone was silent and then, "Okay, Jen. I know how badly you've wanted to hike this trail, but I sure hope you know what you're doing."

After hanging up the phone, I wondered what it had cost her to say that. After the hike ended, I had to find out. I asked her how she felt the moment she realized I planned to finish the trail.

"Scared for you," she replied. "Quite scared. But when your father and I first married, he said I was not to hold back the children because of my own fears. He always wanted you kids free to explore and figure out what you were capable of without any hindrance from me. I lived by that, even when it was difficult."

She went on to explain that, as a young woman, she suffered anxieties about being in large crowds, speaking on the telephone and other situations. She hadn't wanted to pass on those fears to her children and readily agreed to my father's request. I was deeply surprised; I never suspected my mother held such fears. She always seemed so strong to me, and she was — but just not in the way I thought.

Around seven that evening Pete Chadwick, of Pipestone Mountaineering in Butte, arrived and he hurried through the introductions, excited to show us what he had brought. Pulling the bivy sack out of its blue-gray bag, he unfurled it with one flick of his wrist. It lay on the floor like a long, empty trash bag.

I thought: If that's what I'm going to sleep in for the next two months, I may have made a mistake.

Pete slid the fiberglass poles into the palm of one hand and showed me how he had taped the ends of four of them to designate one set of poles, leaving the remaining three as another set.

"I hope you don't mind my doing that," he said.

I did, but I didn't say so. I would wait to see if his tape markings were useful. If not, I would remove them.

Pete inserted the hoops, and I slid my sleeping bag into the sack, squirming in after it. He hovered over me, pointing out the zippering system sunroof and how to sleep in the rain without suffocating.

Greg sat on the bed, grinning.

We bought the sack, and I thanked Pete for his help. He neatly folded the credit card slip, looked around the room a final time and asked Greg if he was ready to go.

Startled, I interrupted, "Do you mind if I have a minute alone with him?"

"Oh, of course. Yeah, I'll just, ah, wait in the truck, all right? Well, good luck then." He shook my hand and left.

"This is the big moment," Greg teased, awkward in his departure. He was dressed in his town clothes, wind pants and tevas, fleece neatly zippered. He opened his arms, and I slid into his embrace.

Holding him tight, sadness rose up in my throat, then stopped, stuck midway. Dry-eyed, I stepped back and searched for something to say. There didn't seem to be anything meaningful enough to last two months of separation.

He gave me a half smile and hoisted his pack to his shoulder. It was all happening too fast. "I love you, Jen. I'll be thinking of you."

"I love you too, Greg. I'll see you in a couple of months." I hated the words as they came out of my mouth. Surely there was something better to say at a time like this.

I stood by the door as I watched him disappear around the corner. I wanted to shout, "Wait a minute!" But I didn't. What was the point?

I leaned against the door frame and watched as dusk settled. I was alone, completely alone. The buildings turned a soft gray, then black. I listened to a woman call her children in for the night and cars pass on the highway.

Sliding down, I sat on the concrete step. When was the last time I was alone? Reviewing my life, I saw twenty years slip by, during only one of which I wasn't living in a barracks, staff dormitory or with a lover. One year alone, and that had been a decade ago.

I wrapped my arms around my knees, pulling them tight against the cool of the evening. A light switched on in the house across the way and a peace settled over the small town. I took a deep breath and welcomed the silence — and the solitude. Perhaps, like my mother, I had a taste for it.

Chapter 9

Solo Hiker Fears
Wisdom, MT south to Lemhi Pass, MT

Come morning, I put on my pack and walked down the now familiar Main Street of Wisdom. I felt vulnerable in a way I never had when I was with Greg. I imagined everyone was staring at me. In truth, there were few people up that early, and those that were had their own business to pursue.

I walked about a hundred yards out of town before stopping to thumb a ride. It was 32 miles to the trailhead, and I wasn't about to walk all that way. Looking back at the Sunoco station, I saw a man climb into the cab of his truck. I hoped he would give me a ride, but like everyone else, I had heard my share of horror stories about women and hitchhiking — the murders, the rapes, the grizzly things you know will never happen to you, yet happen to someone.

Uncertain, I dropped my arm and started walking. The driver passed me. Watching the back of his pickup, I calculated it would take nine hours to walk to the trail, and I didn't have an extra day's worth of food. I found myself wishing I were a man, imagining that would eliminate these troublesome fears.

"It is broad daylight on a busy road," I coached myself, "And nothing bad is going to happen to me."

When I heard the next car approaching from behind, however, I continued walking, still nervous. Fifteen minutes passed while a dozen or so vehicles swooshed by. Any one of them might have given me a quick ride to the trail, if only I had the courage to hitchhike. Shoot, Jen, it's going to be 5:00 p.m., and you'll still be on this stinking road, I complained to myself.

More angry than afraid, I turned to face the traffic and thrust my thumb in the air. In less than ten minutes, a young man pulled up beside me and began clearing the passenger seat. His face was open, his eyes friendly. I told myself, you can't tell these things by looking, but he doesn't appear to be a rapist. Then I accepted his invitation for a ride.

My map showed a faint trail running from Highway 43 to the Continental Divide at Big Hole Pass. When we crossed the second bridge out of town, I asked him to pull over. The trail should be close by. Unfortunately, so was a ranch house. As odd as this may seem, in the 1,500 miles we had hiked, we had never had to ask permission to walk through someone's land.

What if they said no? Their ranch might spread for miles, taking who knows how long to hike around it. Yet some landowners were annoyed with hikers, their welcome worn thin by years of trespassers. With my stomach tight I walked up their dirt driveway. I considered trying to sneak past but only briefly. In this open landscape, they were sure to see me.

I stepped over the discarded mud boots and dirty pails that cluttered the front porch and knocked. A middle-aged woman answered the door, her flowered blouse neatly tucked into her slacks. She listened attentively and seemed neither disturbed nor interested. She simply nodded yes and gave me directions — down the road, past the barn and keep on going.

I thanked her and left. Her driveway continued behind the house, and I quickly reached the barn, a large wooden building with a front opening that was so large you could have fit their house inside. The driveway petered out, and I followed a trail south into an open pasture.

Prairie grass and sage covered the dusty ground. Barn swallows darted past, calling out in their high-pitched whistles. A river flowed a quarter of a mile to my right and sparse groves of trees grew at its banks.

Smiling, I quickened my pace. It was unlikely I would find anyone else out here, since only one road would cross my trail in the next five days. I was alone at last — except, as I soon discovered, for seventy or eighty young bulls that lived in the pasture.

The river swung closer to my trail, and it was then I saw the black animals grazing among the trees. They appeared to be yearlings, calves from the previous season that were allowed to grow to maturity. The nearest ones were just beginning to notice me; lifting their heads, they stared at me, this curious creature.

Over the months I had learned how to handle cattle — or so I thought. They were usually easily frightened. I glanced again and found nearly all of them were following in my wake. At about this time it occurred to me that my experience with cattle was mostly with cows and calves — not bulls. I searched for a fence and saw one over thirty yards away, and it was all uphill. I considered abandoning my nice trail for the safety of the hilltop.

This is ridiculous, I told myself. I am not going to ruin this hike by being a nervous Nellie over every little thing. I stopped hiking and faced the bulls. They formed a long line across the field — the better to see me; their baffled looks and swishing tails gave the impression they were harmless. Convinced of this, I grew tired of watching them and decided to move on. Before leaving, I impulsively lifted my arms in the air and yelled, "Boooo!"

In unison, the herd charged — and they were coming at me! Dust billowed from their hooves, and the ground shook.

Adrenalin pumped through my veins, as I stood frozen, holding my breath. Of the barrage of thoughts I had in those first seconds, one stood out most clearly: I wished like hell I hadn't shouted.

By the time I realized I better start running for that fence, I felt a change in the herd. As a whole they lacked conviction, turned away, and the lead bulls veered off, puzzled about where everyone else was going. Soon they were all milling about, grazing and drifting back to the river. Relieved, I took a shaky breath and hurried on, eager to at last be on my way to Montana's Bitterroot Range.

It was dusk by the time I reached Big Hole Pass, bone tired from backpacking fourteen hours. Sleet and rain had followed me into the mountains, and black water streamed down the trunks of ponderosa pine and Douglas fir.

Huddled under a low branch against the weather, I was waiting for a pot of water to boil over my gas stove. I turned on my headlamp and removed the lid from the pot: steam but no bubbles. Replacing the lid, I snapped off the light. The sound of the gas stove was mild comfort as I sat on the damp ground, arms wrapped around my knees, thinking.

Though it wasn't uncommon for Greg and I to hike separately, each adrift in our own thoughts, we always came together for dinner, and he always cooked. A sudden ache filled my chest. He was probably at his first stop on his way home to New York. I glanced at my watch: 9:10 p.m. He would have arrived in Lander around one in the afternoon. He had probably taken a shower and gone out with our friends for an early dinner. I pictured them back at the house, sitting around the kitchen table drinking tea, our friends' big yellow cat curled up in Greg's lap.

The water began to boil. I lifted the lid to my pot and tossed in the usual pasta, freeze-dried beef and tomato powder. Several minutes later I turned off the stove and ate one more spaghetti dinner alone. Afterward, I hung my food and pack far from my sleeping bag. After returning, I tugged the edge of the bivy sack closer to a fallen tree trunk. I hoped the tree would discourage animals from walking there, reducing my odds of being stepped on during the night.

Still, as I lay on the ground with nothing but a thin sheet of Gore-Tex between my sleeping bag and everything out there, I shrunk even closer to the tree. The night was so very dark, the stars hidden, and my eyes and ears searched the rain-soaked forest for approaching bears. I remembered a story Greg had read to me before setting out on the CDT. It told of two hikers who searched out a foul smell and found the body of a camper, mauled to death by a grizzly. I wondered if the camper had seen it coming.

Talk about lonely! Suddenly my mind was peeling back the years, returning me to my childhood, the thrill of my first campout with the Brownies. But the memory of Greg's story returned, the camper dead — killed by a bear.

I closed my eyes and tried to stop thinking, stop listening. My imagination dismissed the joys of childhood, as if it had never happened, picked up speed and began to run wild, reminding me of camping years ago, when I was so frightened that the best I could do was sleep in my van with doors locked and windows tightly shut, sweltering in the heat. Then there was the night I was the only visitor staying at a huge campground; I had frightened myself with images of men smashing the windows, reaching in and grabbing me. My throat had tightened with fear; and while coughing and choking, I struggled for breath, tears pouring down my face.

Later, a friend suggested my anxiety attack was caused by the stories I told myself. Scary stories would leave me scared, peaceful ones peaceful. Driven by my intense desire to be outdoors, I gradually re-wrote my stories. When I replayed that night in the campground, instead of imagining a truck full of drunken men coming to harass me, I pictured the same truck with two rangers checking on my safety. Rather than hearing the smashing of windows and rude shouts, I recalled waking to sunlight streaming through the front windshield, birds calling cheerfully.

I got to the point where I was willing to camp again, and each time my imagination conjured a fearful image, I replaced it with a peaceful one. Eventually, I felt comfortable enough to leave the windows cracked for fresh air. Soon I was sleeping in a tent next to my parked van, thrilled to be on the ground.

I wanted to see the stars when I woke at night, to feel the breeze on my face, smell the earth beside me. One night I put up my tent next to my van and placed my sleeping bag on the bare ground beside it. My plan was to sleep in the open, but if I got too scared I could move into the tent or even the van. Hell, I could drive home if I wanted. But first I would try sleeping outside.

I lay on the ground that night, too nervous to enjoy it much but determined to stick it out. Every sound was an approaching deer, every itch, a tick or spider. My breath was becoming short, and I struggled to think of calming stories. Somehow I dozed off in this state and dreamed.

In my dream a rabbit came down the trail and hopped on my chest. I was frightened that it might bite or claw me; then I realized it was there for me to love and with my love to heal it. So I gently petted the rabbit until it hopped over my shoulder and departed.

A second rabbit jumped on my chest; again, I petted it with love until it too hopped away. A third, a fourth, countless numbers of rabbits came to me for healing. I slept comfortably the rest of the night and never again experienced any significant anxiety while sleeping outdoors. With the rabbit dream fresh in my mind, I rolled over and went to sleep.

The next morning I took a side trail in an effort to follow the penciled markings Gill Gale, the Wisdom Forest Ranger, had scribbled on my map. It petered out two miles later. There was no way I was going back. I had 900 miles to finish and wasn't about to do any of it twice. Besides, it looked like easy walking.

Lodgepole pine shielded the forest floor, preventing the sunlight

needed by all but the most determined shrubs. I decided to hike without
a trail for the remaining four miles to the pass, hoping that for once
bushwhacking would not include climbing over fallen trees, thrashing
through wet mountain laurel or confronting an impassable river. I was
wrong, really wrong!

My open path was soon replaced by thick gooseberry and
elderberry, wet with morning dew. I shoved through, getting soaked
in the process. As the morning wore on I teetered across rockslides
and scrambled up steep slopes. By the time I reached the top I was
sweaty, scratched and ready for the cooling breeze that greeted me.
The sky was clear, and having gained the ridge, I looked forward to
more modest climbs for the remainder of the day.

In the afternoon I came to a clear pond nestled beneath the sharp
rock face of the ridgeline. Sunlight sparkled off its cobalt blue surface.
I checked my bearings on the map and noticed the pond was unnamed.

"I dub ye Lake Jennifer," I declared loudly and wrote the name on
my map. It didn't matter to me that the lake probably *did* have an
official name and was simply omitted from my large-scale map. It was
just plain old fun to claim it as my own. In my opinion there weren't
enough places named after women. Most of the mountains, lakes and
towns that are named after people are named for men: Mt. Marcy, Mt.
Everest, Mt. Whitney, Mt. McKinley, Lake George, Washington D.C.,
Jamestown and so on. "This is all about to change," I boasted aloud
as I put away my pencil.

The next morning I sat on my pack, frowning at my map. In less
than two miles the slope became so steep I couldn't be sure it wasn't
a cliff. If I couldn't cross, I would have to descend to the bottom of the
mountain and climb back up the other side, which — in my opinion —
would be a sinful waste of effort. If only I had been able to locate the

surveyor's markers the ranger had told me about, I wouldn't be in this predicament. But my search the night before for the orange plastic strips had been futile.

Again I studied the contour lines on the map, straining to picture the scene in my mind. It still looked awfully steep. Perhaps I should climb higher and avoid the cliff that way. I studied the craggy peaks of the ridgeline. No, it didn't seem passable. Then I noticed on the map that, farther down the mountain, one section of the cliff appeared slightly less steep, its contour lines spaced farther apart. Perhaps I could cross there. If nothing else, it was worth a closer look.

Using my altimeter, I determined I was 1,200 feet above the area I intended to cross. With that, I made the decision to descend straight down before skirting the slope southwest for a little over a mile.

The morning sun filled the air with a rich, piney scent; and, with each step, pebbles tumbled down the mountainside. An eagle called out. I paused to enjoy the lingering echo of its cry. I searched the skies but couldn't find it. Nevertheless, I said, "Thank you, Lord." The thin prairie grass soon gave way to an increasing number of slate-colored rocks. I stopped and looked up.

From the top of the mountain to far down its slope was a continuous rockslide. It was a quarter of a mile across and consisted of boulders that were one to two feet in diameter. Though I had crossed many rockslides in my travels, I was never comfortable doing so. I always worried I would jar the one rock that would start all of them sliding, crushing me under their weight.

I noticed tufts of grass growing amongst the slide, indicating they had not moved that year. I stepped on a nearby rock, testing its stability. It shifted but held. The stones lay in a jumble, many offering only a thin edge for me to walk on. I teetered on the sharp rocks, my hiking poles scraping their hard surface. Fifteen minutes later my ankles were weary and gnats buzzed around my face. I didn't swat them or slow down. If I stumbled here, the odds of my spraining an ankle or twisting a knee were high.

With sweat stinging my eyes, I looked up and discovered the rockslide ended in another ten feet. I wobbled across the final stretch and stepped gratefully onto firm soil.

Relieved, I took a deep breath and looked into the forest to find my route. To my delight, I spotted a fluorescent orange strip of plastic tied to a branch directly in front of me.

"Hooo-aahhh!" I hollered, pleased that I had picked the same route as the U.S. Forest Service. For the next mile I joyously followed the orange strips tied to branches and tree trunks until they ended at a jeep road. There was no trail on the far side, and I was back to bushwhacking.

That night raindrops awakened me. It was around two in the morning. I heard the rain in the forest and smelled the rich wetness of it. Unfortunately, I couldn't just pull the hood of the bivy sack over my face. I hadn't assembled the poles the night before, the ones Pete, the retailer, had so carefully marked for me. It would have taken only a few minutes. But I had hiked until after dark, and I was chewed up by mosquitoes, nearly out of drinking water, spooked by the empty forest and feeling sorry for myself. Tomorrow was my thirty-eighth birthday, and I would be spending it alone. Skipping the chore of threading my poles through the hood was about the only pleasure I had. As with most vices, I now had plenty of time to regret it.

The rain fell harder. I gripped the edge of the hood and tried to hold it at the proper angle to keep out the water. It worked — but soon my arms tired from holding them in the air. I stuffed spare clothes under my elbows, and managed to brace up my arms. My fingers soon grew stiff. Nonetheless, I drifted off to sleep.

The sagging of my arms jerked me awake. While wondering if I could continue to hold them up while asleep, I drifted off again. For thirty minutes I dozed in short spurts as I waited for the rain to stop. It didn't.

I decided to put up the hoops and get some real sleep. Still in my sleeping bag, I pulled my rain jacket out of my pillow sack and thrashed about before getting the jacket on and zippered to my chin. I squirmed out of my bivy sack as quickly as I could, then jumped up and covered my sleeping bag with the collapsed fabric. My jacket was getting soaked, but at least my bag would be dry.

My bare feet cringed from the wet, rough ground as I hurried to the tree where I hung my pack. Feeling for the tiny slice of duct tape at the end of the poles, I assembled the hoops in the dark and threaded them through the hood.

Thank you, Pete, I thought, for the little tape markings.

Finished, I ripped off my rain jacket and folded it inside out before jumping into my sleeping bag. Though I was damp and shivering, the thick down quickly warmed me, and I fell asleep with the rain pounding on my now taut hood. Never again was I tempted to skip that chore.

In the morning I sang a cheerless *Happy Birthday*, ate a candy bar for breakfast and headed south. It had stopped raining in the night, and the ridge was washed clean and quiet. The trail was easy to follow. All I lacked was water and Greg.

I reached Lemhi Pass around noon, walked twenty feet out of my way to read a billboard commemorating the first crossing of the Continental Divide by the Lewis and Clark Expedition and then hiked down the west road in search of water. I hadn't found any in nearly twenty-four hours. The map showed a spring within fifty feet of the pavement, but I saw nothing. I continued walking — begrudging every step I took downhill, knowing I would have to retrace it back up. Then I heard a faint trickle.

I stopped and searched the wooded hillside. Deep gullies rippled across the slope, obscured by thick brush and stubby pines. I didn't see any sign of water, but I heard a clear gurgling sound. I plunged into the nearest gully, climbed the far side and wandered deeper into the forest, first losing, then regaining the sound of the spring. Finally, I spotted it!

Dropping my pack, I filled a pot of water and put it on the stove to boil. Having done that, I remembered the knots Greg had taught me, or at least something close to them, and strung a rope between two trees. I hung my damp sleeping bag and bivy sack over the sagging line and stepped back to admire my achievement.

None of what I had done was difficult, but the simple tasks of finding water, drying my gear and cooking lunch revived my flagging spirits. I pulled out my notepad and wrote a long letter to my friend, Bethany. It was then I knew that I was going to be all right — even on the tough days.

Chapter 10

The Kindness of Strangers
Lemhi Pass, MT south to Morrison Lake, MT

Come evening I set up camp atop a ridge among a few shrubby pine trees. They offered scant protection from the high winds, but water and the trail were nearby. By the time I was ready for sleep, the sun was just starting to set. I lay on my left side and watched it edge closer to the horizon. Soon my eyes were burning; I flipped to the other side — just in time to see the full moon rising in the east. The moon was blood orange and bigger than I ever remembered seeing it. I stared in awe. Glancing over my shoulder, I peeked at the setting sun, thrilled to experience those two beautiful sights at the same time.

I longed to share this with Greg, the ooohing and aaahing together that would make it so special. Being alone had its own appeal, though. It seemed almost like a private show, a gift created for me. "Thank you, Lord," I said. "Thank you for the birthday present."

By nine the next morning I had hiked six miles, alternating between grassland and white bark pine, my route littered with Indian paintbrush, bistort and pygmy bitterroot, a small reddish flower that hugged the ground in the middle of the road.

The sky was clear, the trail gentle and the view gorgeous. Mountains spilled in every direction: the Beaverhead Mountains, the Maiden Peak line of summits, the rugged Italian Peaks, nearby Goat Mountain, and finally the Lemhi Range and Lemhi Valley. I was so filled with joy that I burst into song:

> Ho, ho, ho, ho, Life is good to me.
> Ho, ho, ho, ho, Life is good to me.
> Ho, ho, ho, ho, Life is good to me.
> I never will forget that Life is good to me..

At the end of the verse, I slammed my trekking poles in unison with the clapping of my imaginary congregation and belted out another round. I kept repeating the simple verse until the euphoria passed, leaving a glow of contentment in its wake.

I couldn't remember the last time I had felt so good, so alive. It was as though I could reach out either hand and touch a mountain top, leap as high as the clouds or glide on the back of the cool breeze, delighting in the green and brown carpeted mountains below. Being alone in the mountains, it seemed, had brought out this dizzy happiness, and I vowed to spend a week hiking solo every year of my life, no matter how my husband and kids might object. I needed it. Perhaps we all need time to be free, time alone in nature, supported and encouraged to discover our own wild selves, to reconnect with who we are and what we want from life.

Perhaps we all needed to come away feeling confident and empowered, blessed by the grace of the sunlight, wind, moon, water and mountain tops — purified by the high altitude air.

So few of us realize it, fewer still act on it, women especially.

When I was a Ridge Runner for the Appalachian Mountain Club, I lived on the Appalachian Trail, helping hikers, monitoring trail conditions and enforcing AMC camping policies. Every weekend I would inevitably encounter two to three Boy Scout troops. Yet not once did I come across a group of girls hiking the trail, let alone backpacking.

This lack of exposure to the woods as children surely must contribute to the nearly total absence of teen and young adult women from the trails. It seems the few women who backpack are those who are lucky enough to have a boyfriend or husband to teach them.

What are we stealing from our girls with this omission? Their very birthright should be to feel at home in the natural world, embraced by its cyclical rhythms and blessed by its wild beauty. And what are we depriving the wilderness? Feminine stewardship might possibly introduce a more gentle and inclusive management of our natural resources. Women, with their natural inclination toward interdependency with all species, are as important to preserving the Earth as men, the champions of decisive action. But how can that happen when girls and women have never slept in a forest, let alone gained enough skills to do so alone, thereby tasting the power of their own wild nature?

I walked into Bannock Pass the following morning, my end point for this section. Forest Service Road 29 was a well maintained, gravel road that crossed the pass, connecting the small towns of Grant, Montana and Leadore, Idaho. The later was my next resupply point, fourteen miles to the south.

I had read that traffic was sparse through Bannock Pass, but never did I suspect it would be so bad. I waited nearly twenty minutes before seeing a vehicle of any sort — a jeep headed in the wrong direction. After the wind swept away its dust cloud, I put more sun block on my arms and sipped from my nearly empty water bottle. Realizing I might not get a ride, I began walking toward town. It would take most of the day, but I might not have a choice.

A half-hour later I heard an engine laboring over the pass. It was a truck pulling a camper. I stuck out my thumb with slim hope. It seemed ironic to me that vacationers, the people with the most leisure time available, were among the least likely to help me out. Angry at the thought that someone might leave me on this barren road, I stepped to its center, feet spread wide and arms waving over my head.

Given the choice of either running me over or stopping, they stopped. The woman slowly rolled down the passenger window. I explained my situation in a cheerful but urgent manner.

Looking to her husband for reassurance, she reluctantly nodded her head. I climbed into their back seat and set my pack beside me. The air conditioner blasted cool air as my eyes adjusted to the window-tinted darkness. It felt heavenly.

We sped swiftly out of the pass and wound through the lower slopes of the range. Hearing I was from New York, they launched into a well-rehearsed lecture about easterners, environmentalists and meddlers in general. I didn't care. I had a ride and would soon be in my motel room, drinking an ice cold Diet Coke.

As we neared town, the rocky cliffs gave way to rolling hills and dry ranch land. The Forest Service road ended at the highway, and I thanked them for the lift and returned to walking.

The town center was a row of buildings set off from the pavement by barren parking lots and sagebrush fields. Behind me were a handful of houses. In front was a gas station where I picked up sodas, candy bars and directions to the Leadore Inn.

Unfortunately, I had arrived a day early, and all four rooms of the Inn were filled. Feeling badly about turning me away, the owner, Aleta Ries, encouraged me to go across the street to Lema's RV park. Then she added, "I hope you don't mind, but my husband and I picked up your mail yesterday. It seemed like quite a few packages for you to carry all the way from the Post Office."

I assured her it was more than fine — it was great.

She rushed on, "All right, if you give me a minute, I'll help you carry it over."

I'll give you an hour, I thought, grinning.

She soon came around the end of the building, arms loaded with packages. "Here," she said, "you start across with these, and I'll get the rest."

The tiny office of the RV park was filled with a single island of shelves bulging with chips and popcorn, candy bars and nuts. The surrounding walls carried a wide range of groceries and camping supplies. Next to the door was a short counter, behind which were piles of newspapers, cigarette cartons, a cash register and a woman. She was seated on a high stool and reading a magazine when I walked through the door.

"Can I help you?" she asked.

We worked out the details of my stay, and I paid for the privilege of camping on her lawn. At least I got a hot shower out of it. She absentmindedly accepted my two dollars while studying the registration form I filled out.

"You're alone?" She frowned. "There isn't anyone with you?"

"That's right; my husband had to stop."

"Isn't that dangerous — hiking by yourself?"

Her question annoyed me. She didn't sound impressed at all, only concerned, something I hadn't heard in the four months I hiked with Greg. Perhaps as she implied, her worries were simply about a person hiking solo, but I doubted it. If I were a man, she would probably be awed by my bravery and obvious skill, and would have given a sympathetic nod when she heard my wife had dropped out. Instead, I was treated like I was in grave danger and foolishly blind to the fact.

Over the next few weeks I found this was nearly always the response I got, particularly from other women. It was depressing to see what little faith we have in ourselves.

I spread out my tent and sleeping bag to dry in the sun, sat on her lawn and opened my mail. I arranged the colorful collection of birthday cards and gifts on the grass before me and felt the last vestiges of loneliness slip away as I read and re-read their letters. Every once in a while I would stop and gaze at the Centennial Mountains that rose gracefully before me. My eyes scanned the sage-covered hills for antelope while I slowly ate homemade fudge brownies and chocolate covered cranberries.

The coin laundry looked like a shed from the highway, built at the end of a duplex parking lot. Aside from the wind pants and fleece jacket I had on, I put all my clothes into the washer and turned on the half-filled load. I sat down beside the dryer and began writing letters.

Just after I moved the clothes to the dryer, Aleta swung open the door. "Greg called the Inn," she announced. "Hop in the truck, and I'll give you a ride. Don't worry about your laundry. No one will bother it here."

I climbed into her truck, and she pulled onto the empty highway. Aleta looked to be in her early thirties, and I wondered if she had any kids. She would make a good Mom; she was patient and giving.

"Did he leave a number?" I asked.

"Yeah, but he won't be there long. He's got somewhere to go. You can call from my house."

I began to protest.

She cut me off. "I saw someone on the pay phone when I drove past." She leaned forward, peering through her windshield. "Yep, he's still on it."

Sure enough, a man leaned into the booth outside the gas station.

"How did you find me?" I asked.

"Oh, that wasn't hard." She slowed down and turned into her driveway. "My friend said you left the RV park some time ago with your laundry bag. I called the café, store and Post Office to see if I could catch you along the way. None of them had seen you, so I knew that was where you were."

I called the number Greg had left with her, and he answered after the first ring. He sounded rushed, but I supposed that was just normal New York speed, while I was still on laid-back hiker time. The tale of his journey home was covered swiftly, followed by a flurry of activity in the two days hence. He was staying with friends until my return and was even now getting ready to go out to dinner with them. I was glad. At least he wasn't alone and miserable.

When it came my turn to fill him in I found it a lot tougher than I had imagined. I couldn't share with him as I always had. He hadn't been there. He didn't know the Bitterroots. And no matter how hard I tried to describe the disappearing trails, dry ridges and cold rain, I couldn't get back the feeling that we were doing it together.

"Jen, that sounds tough," he tried to be sympathetic. I tapped the pen against Aleta's desk and wished I were back with my laundry. "Yeah, well, you know how it is. You do what you've got to do. Look, I better let you go. Don't want to keep your friends waiting."

"They can wait. I only get to speak to my wife once a week now." Nonetheless, we ran out of things to say, and in a couple of minutes he hung up.

I sat in the air-conditioned office, staring at the foothills north of Leadore and feeling more alone than ever.

That night a blazing full moon and honking geese awakened me. I was so hungry I couldn't imagine waiting until the café opened at six, but I fell back asleep. Three hours later I was across the street in Deb's Sagebrush Café enjoying a double order of cinnamon French toast.

After eating, I cleared my own table and then spread out my maps. I overheard several men discussing the rising cost of hay. One rancher was selling it for seventy dollars, uncut, mostly to outfitters. They all agreed it was a bad year.

"How come?" My question rang through the nearly empty room. There was silence.

Then the man who had been speaking turned to me. "Too much

rain," he answered. "The longest dry spell this spring was five days."
He held up four fingers and a thumb to emphasize his point.

"Boy," I said and shook my head.

I can't remember where I read that the only way to travel is alone.
With another you become a crowd, bringing with you your own world
— missing the world around you. If Greg had been there, I never would
have talked to those old guys. Now that I had, it was like we were all
sitting at the same table.

By nine o'clock in the morning, I was loading my pack into Aleta's
pick-up. When she had offered to give me a ride back to Bannock
Pass, I readily accepted. In addition to retrieving my mail, fetching me
when Greg called and offering me this ride, Aleta had sewn my gaiters
and invited me into her home to meet her husband, Mike Ries. As we
headed north through the foothills, I asked her why she had gone out
of her way to help me so much.

"I like helping hikers," she began. "It feels good. I moved to Leadore
five years ago. Only seventy-five people live here, and it's nice and
quiet. When I go to visit my sister in Tacoma she is so busy with work
and the kids, and driving back and forth everywhere, she doesn't have
time for people anymore." She looked at me, searching for understanding.
"Don't get me wrong, my sister is very loving, but she's so busy, we
don't really get to visit." She paused. "My husband and I, we decided
we didn't want to live like that. We always want to have time for family,
friends and people like you, who're just passing through."

She stopped talking and silence filled the cab as I reflected on
what she said. Knowing that I, too, often lead a hectic life back home,
I vowed to learn from Aleta and to make time for others, even strangers.

Afternoon found me following a faint trail, six miles to the summit
of Elk Mountain. Picking my way through the rocky mound at its top,

I looked over my shoulder to check the dark clouds coming toward me from the west. It was three in the afternoon, and I watched lightning streak to the ridge where I had been hiking only an hour earlier.

The cool breeze dried my sweat as I sipped from my water bottle and gazed at the panorama of summits before me. I calmly watched the storm approach. I wasn't too concerned, guessing that it would linger on the peak long after I left. Daring myself to stay as long as possible, I waited until the driving wind became thick with raindrops before quickly hiking down the eastern slope.

The storm did settle on the peak, and I continued my hike under a cloudless sky. An hour later I reached a saddle, a low point between two hilltops. It didn't feel right. It didn't make sense to be climbing again when I should be dropping into the Centennial Valley, and I was low on water.

I pulled out my map and GPS. In Leadore the forest ranger, Norma Staaf, had penciled a large X where she remembered seeing a spring. Though I vaguely knew where that might be, the rolling slopes of the mountain concealed the true lay of the land and I relied more on guessing than science in figuring out my route.

I set off across the open slope, surrounded by a profusion of lupine, dandelion, yarrow and clover. I passed in and out of white bark pine stands and traversed up and down hills. None of it was different from what I left behind. I was beginning to wonder if I was going in circles when I topped a small rise. Directly in front of me was a cattle trough. Fresh spring water flowed over its wooden planks and soaked into the ground.

I called out, "Thank you, Lord!" I figured I would never have found the spring without help.

The next morning I woke to the sound of a chattering red squirrel. I opened my eyes to discover him bathed in sunlight on a pine tree branch directly above me. I reached under my pillow for my running shorts and stopped.

This is it, I thought. *This* is my hike.

I strove to etch it into my memory, all of it, the red squirrel, the sun-filled pine, the cool air on my face and the eagerness I felt to hike another day on the Continental Divide. It didn't matter to me whether it rained, I got lost or I couldn't find water. I still looked forward to it. I had all day to hike through the mountains with just myself, the sun, the wind —

"And you stinkin', noisy squirrels!" I shouted with a laugh.

Chapter 11

Ghost Town Jitters
Morrison Lake, MT south to Mack's Inn, ID

I had just broken camp at Pileup Canyon. I was headed to Medicine Lodge Pass when I paused to sit on the side of a jeep road and remove my wind pants over my boots. I hadn't quite gotten the pants off when a pick-up truck carrying a four-wheeler stopped in front of me.

Thank God I have on my running shorts, I thought.

The driver rolled down the passenger window. "Where you headed?" he asked.

I assumed he owned or leased this land, stopping as much to pass the time as to check out a trespasser. "I'm hiking the Continental Divide Trail from Mexico to Canada," I said. "Got about eight hundred miles to go." I pointed up the road to the top of the ridge. "The Leadore Forest Ranger said the CDT should be up there somewhere."

"Yeah, it's up there; just follow the jeep road, and you shouldn't have any problems."

Later I had to wonder if we were talking about the same trail.

Our conversation fell into a comfortable lull and like two workers on a coffee break we took our time in picking it up again.

"I suppose you're treating your water?" He glanced sideways to see my response.

I nodded.

He described how a fellow from New Jersey had been admitted to the hospital after drinking untreated water from Big Sheep Creek. He had seen locals doing that and decided he could do the same. He was wrong. He ended up contracting an intestinal bug and lost forty pounds in two weeks.

I asked about the antelope hunters, and he told me about rescuing men from Colorado, Texas and all over the country who were lost or injured hunting in the Bitterroot Range. He said it without rancor or disdain, but I couldn't help but think these Montana ranchers would be better off with a little less company.

I could have listened to his stories much longer, but after ten minutes or so, our conversation wound down, as though on some unspoken cue.

"Well, guess I better get back to work," he said. "Got a lot of area to cover today."

Impulsively, I extended my hand. "It's nice to meet you. By the way, my name's Jennifer Allen."

He shook my hand. "Mike Matthews. Take care of yourself, Jennifer. Don't worry, you'll make it."

Long after his dust had settled and I was pushing to the ridge, his final words echoed in my thoughts, "Don't worry, you'll make it." In the ten days I had been hiking alone, he was the first person, aside from Greg, who expressed confidence instead of fear about my hiking the trail.

As I stepped off the jeep road and headed west along the ridge top, I called out, "Thanks, Mike!" as if he might be in hearing distance.

My way was made easy by the worn dirt track that ran along the spine of the Continental Divide. Within a short distance, however, I noticed a wooden post standing in the grassy slope below me. Curious, I hiked to it. On it was the freshly painted emblem of the CDT. It was the first I had seen in over a thousand miles!

Was I willing to give up my nice jeep road for the novelty of hiking on the actual Continental Divide Trail? There were plenty of reasons to say no. The trail wasn't marked on my map. There was little tread to follow; there were no other sign posts in sight; and, there was no telling how far it went before it ended, possibly without warning. But someone had made an effort to cut the trail. The least I could do was use it.

I set off across the slope, my ankles straining with the effort. At the next rise I saw no evidence of either another CDT post or trail. Though I was agitated by how widely spaced the markers were, I decided to hike a little farther and see if a post stood over the next hill. None did. Worse yet, the valley was filled with a thick growth, four feet high and a hundred feet deep. My trekking poles were able only to hold back the largest of branches, while my bare thighs and arms took the brunt of the scratching. I pressed on and emerged scratched, sweaty and pissed off.

I dropped down the hill to a stream, washed off the blood and spotted an animal trail. In a half-mile it ended, and I followed a rough compass bearing through a forested gully. When it, too, ended and I stood overlooking yet another valley, I was surprised to see my second CDT post.

Grateful to be back on track, I followed it carefully. In spite of this, it soon took on the meandering contours of an animal trail and, sure enough, ended at a stream. I trudged on, skeptical of the CDT markers that had lured me from the ridge; yet, I remained hopeful I would spot another.

Four hours later, I flung my pack against a rock and sat on it. To hell with the CDT, I thought, I'll find my own trail. I pulled out my maps and looked for a pack trail going my way. Earlier that day I had seen a group of horse packers, three riders trailing two mules loaded with gear. Judging by the small size of the group, I suspected they were local ranchers checking their fences. In any event, where there were horses there were usually pack trails. Sometimes they were even marked on the map.

I was tracing my route around Garfield Mountain when I heard loud thrashing to my left. A large animal burst from the trees. A mule, I thought, then realized my mistake. Less than thirty feet away stood a bull moose. Without hesitation he galloped across the open field, his dark chocolate hide glistening over long, sinewy muscles. He reminded me of a stallion as he quickly crossed the meadow and dropped into the streambed on its far side.

I sat in awe, maps and lost trails forgotten. I had never seen a moose run before. In fact, I had always seen them grazing in ponds or marshy fields and had come to think of them as clumsy, oversized deer. But that moose was not clumsy in the least. He was beautiful! "Thank you, Lord!" I called out in triumph.

I followed a well-defined pack trail around Garfield Mountain, was chased off a ridge by lightning, and around five o'clock that evening reached Sawmill Creek. Though I still had a few hours of daylight, I impulsively decided to camp. It didn't make sense — not really. I was in a valley with a flat, easy walk along the creek with plenty of nice spots to camp. But I simply felt like stopping. So, stop I did.

I had set up my bivy sack and was starting up the stove when big drops of rain plopped from the sky. Within minutes it became a downpour. I dove into my sleeping bag and popped up the hood of my bivy sack. The storm thrashed the sagebrush field, and I delighted in the scent and feel of it, its sheer power invigorating me.

My near escape seemed too coordinated to be a coincidence. I must have sensed the storm coming. It seemed the gulf between nature's rhythms and my actions was shrinking. A harmony was being struck, a blending of forces. Without conscious effort I was beginning to feel my way along the Divide.

I reached the town of Monida, Montana the afternoon of the next day. It wasn't officially a ghost town; some people still lived there. But it felt like one. Monida stretched a thousand yards north to south and three blocks deep. Its pine board and cinder block buildings were lifeless — once colorful locations covered with dust and soot.

I hurried through the empty streets, anxious to put the town behind me. On its outskirts a group of houses, made shabby and small by the prairie, dwarfed their dingy lots. All but one appeared abandoned. It stood on the nearest corner with a sun-scorched truck out front. T-shirts and underwear flapped in the wind on a clothesline.

I considered asking for water. I hadn't found any in over six miles, and my bottle was nearly empty. As I studied the house, I thought I noticed a curtain move. Of course, it could have been a cat or a dog. But what if it was the owner and they were sitting behind that window watching my every move? The hairs on the back of my neck rose.

I continued walking. Just as I was leaving town, I spotted a fair-sized mud puddle in the ditch. It held more than enough water for me, and I reached into my pouch for the iodine tablets. Then I stopped and looked up. The house with the clothesline was in plain view. Were they still watching me? What would they think if they saw me scooping water out of a ditch? Would they call the police?

Unnerved, I closed my pouch and hurried onward. I would just have to find water elsewhere.

By late afternoon I had shooed cows away from a filthy cattle trough, boiled seep water in the 90-degree sun and eaten the dust of commuters speeding toward Interstate 15 from the heart of the Centennial Valley. Furthermore, two converging lightning storms toyed with the idea of coming my way, and the gravel road stretched flat and straight for over thirty miles through private land.

Feeling as though I had been on this road forever — and had forever to go — I plopped down on my pack and gazed at my map. It was now four-thirty in the afternoon, and I just wanted the day to be over.

Traffic was sparse. I watched the approach of a white cargo van for quite some time. It stopped on the road in front of me.

"You lost?" the driver asked, a teasing look in his eye.

I shook my head no, not wanting to encourage more questions.

"Need any water?"

I looked up and down the road. There was no one in sight.

"No, I'm all right. Thanks, though." Still he didn't leave.

"Where you headed?" His thin, gnarled hand lay gently on his side mirror.

Maybe he was just a lonely guy. "Up a ways," I gestured vaguely. "I'll camp when I get tired."

"There's a beautiful campground that way," he said. "The Red Rock Lakes Campground in the wildlife refuge. It's on the left side of the road. You shouldn't have any trouble finding it."

I nodded.

He continued, undeterred by my silence: "I used to be a forest ranger in this area, covered the entire valley as well as the Bearhead Mountains northeast of here. Now I'm retired and live with my daughter up in Missoula. She needed her space, so I packed up a couple of weeks ago and came back for a visit." He looked across the valley. "How about you? What are you doing out here?"

I stood up and put on my pack. If he wasn't going to leave, I was. "I'm hiking the Continental Divide Trail. Been at it since April first and figure I've got about eight hundred miles to finish."

"Alone?" he asked.

It seemed ludicrous to lie; we were in the middle of a very big, very empty valley. If I wasn't alone, my hiking partners sure were a long way off. "Yeah, my husband dropped out a couple weeks ago; injured foot."

"Whoa, and you're hiking without him?" He sounded impressed.

"Yeah, well, I better get going. Still have a few miles to do."

He wished me well and, to my relief, drove off. I glanced over my shoulder to see what progress the nearest lightning storm had made, then turned to find him backing his van toward me.

"Now this may seem like a totally crazy idea," he said when he pulled up beside me, "and if you don't want to do it, that would be just fine, but if you would oblige me, I'd like to take you to Lima and buy you dinner. You can stay the night in town, and I'll drive you back in the morning. Or," he hurried on, "I'll drive you back tonight. Of course, its thirty miles one way, and it'll be after dark by then. But what do you think? Would you like a hot meal?"

Every warning bell I had was going off, yet I stared down at my boots, considering. I couldn't help but picture an ice-cold Coke and hot, dripping burger, and with the miserable day I'd had, they seemed especially appealing.

"What kind of food they got?" I asked.

He smiled and climbed out of the van to help me with my gear. When he slid open the side door, I saw his mattress and clothes, and changed my mind. But I was too slow. He pitched my pack and poles in the back and slammed the door shut. Thrusting his hand before him, he said, "Hi. I'm Hu Humes."

I shook his hand and climbed into the passenger seat.

On the long drive to Lima, Hu told me of his work as a forest ranger and filled me in on the lives of his son, daughter and two-year old grandson. He seemed starved for conversation, and I didn't mind being a good listener. By the time we reached Lima, I was feeling more relaxed. The diner was on our right, but instead Hu made a left turn into the parking lot of a motel.

What the hell? I thought.

"I'd like to clean up before dinner," he said. "Do you mind?"

I shrugged and sank back into my seat.

He got out and fumbled around in the back, presumably getting his clothes together. Finished, he walked past me toward the motel, my backpack on his shoulder.

I leaped out of the van. "Hey, where are you going with that?"

He leaned the pack against the building and turned facing me, arms up in a gesture of innocence. "Don't get excited now. I just thought you might want a hot shower. Of course, if you don't, we can go eat right now." He opened the door to a motel room, stepped sideways onto the porch and eased into a chair ten feet from the door.

It occurred to me I probably smelled to high heaven; this might be his way of discreetly pointing that out, but still I was wary.

He pulled a cigarette from his shirt pocket and said, "But if you'd like to use the shower, go ahead, and I'll wait right here."

Hu lit up his cigarette and stared across the barren parking lot.

I glanced into the darkened room, then watched him again. Aside from lifting the cigarette to and from his mouth, he hadn't moved.

Without a word I picked up my pack, walked into the room and locked the door behind me. My heart was racing as I dug out my fleece and wind pants. Outside, he scraped the chair on the cement porch. I froze, listening, but he didn't come to the door. I went into the tiny bathroom and locked myself in.

Hurrying, I stripped and got in the shower. The hot water poured over my face and shoulders, sweeping away four days of salt, dust and grime. Using the motel's cheap washcloth and tiny bar of soap, I scrubbed myself from top to bottom. It felt wonderful. Afterward, I combed my hair with my fingers and brushed my teeth.

Two years earlier, I had met a woman who was thru-hiking the Appalachian Trail and claimed to have had a hot shower nearly every day of her hike. I don't know how she did it. The sheer logistics of getting on and off the trail that frequently is mind-boggling, but aside from that I wouldn't even want a shower every day. Not because I liked being dirty, but because I would have to leave the trail to get it.

I felt it even as I climbed into Hu's van, and we drove to the diner. That nebulous feeling of being at home in the woods, an animal among animals, trusting myself and my instincts, all of that seemed far away, a fond memory. I knew that later I would probably toss and turn in my sleeping bag, the caffeine keeping me awake; and in the morning the scent of soap would fill my nostrils, blocking the smell of an approaching storm or nearby animal.

Fainter still was a vague feeling that I was betraying something precious. Though I would have been hard pressed to articulate it at the time, each stop in town disrupted my tenuous process of getting to know myself. Every day alone in the mountains I was making decisions about what I wanted, which trail to take, what to eat, when to stop and so on. It was exhilarating. After thirty-eight years of being barraged by society's expectations and the needs of family and friends, I was finally free to discover what I truly wanted.

Returning to town, no matter how briefly, reinforced all the old *shoulds* and *have-tos* and rendered my own answers fuzzy and irrelevant. I think, if I could, I would have stayed on the trail and never gone into town; though I doubt I could have been as strong as Ulysses — overcoming the sirens of a hot shower and Diet Coke.

True to his word, Hu bought me dinner and took me back to the trail that night. Like he said, no funny business. I waved goodbye, and he was gone — a nice old guy who had just been looking for conversation.

Two days later I hiked into Mack's Inn, Idaho and stopped at the resort after which the town was named. My cabin was at the end of a long row and contained a bed, table, chair and a shower that took so long to get hot I walked all the way back to the office to report it not working.

At the Post Office I learned my supply box from home had not arrived. The postmistress explained that mail had been delayed because of a UPS strike. I should check back tomorrow, and if it still wasn't in, surely they would have it after the weekend. "On Tuesday," she said as an afterthought, reminding me that they were closed for Labor Day.

Frustrated, I left the Post Office debating whether I could purchase what I needed and skip town before the package arrived. Finding food and maps would be difficult in a town that only had one small convenience store, but the real dilemma would be replacing the Yellowstone Park permit that was in my box. That would require hitch-hiking 40-plus miles north to West Yellowstone, finding the back country office open, convincing them to re-issue my permit, then possibly hitch-hiking south to Dubois to buy food and maps, and finally catching a ride back to Mack's Inn. It seemed like too much hassle on a day off.

I drifted back to my cabin, comforted by the familiar routine of town chores. The package didn't arrive on Saturday, and I spent the day inside, content to make hot chocolate on my stove while rain splashed on the windowsill.

I pulled out my notepad and entered the date, August 22.

I think I'll start journaling more and writing fewer letters. I want to really hear myself on this journey, and I think that's one of the best ways.

The woman at the snack bar had been incredulous that I was walking alone. "Aren't you afraid?"

I usually said, "No," but I think from now on I'm going to ask, "Of what?"

By afternoon I was getting restless. I wrote:

I want to hike. I want to feel the sure, swift movements of packing my gear and heading into the mountains. I want to be 20 miles farther tonight than this morning. If I had my food box, maps and permit I would be out of here. God's will. God's timing. Not mine.

In the morning I went to The Church in the Pines, a one room building with a seating capacity of eighty. The pine board walls had no insulation, and the tiny congregation squeezed past the empty wood-burning stove that stood in the middle of the aisle.

I nodded at a woman who smiled at me and took my seat near an open window. Pine boughs danced in the stormy breeze; I imagined myself standing beneath them, head tilted back, gazing up at their colorful performance. I struggled to capture the words to describe how I felt. It was as though I wasn't watching the branches; rather, that a part of me was up in the tree with them. No, it was more than that. I felt a part of me *was* the pine bough, and I was the wind that pushed it, as well. I was the raindrops that fell from the sky and the soft sand that absorbed them.

Seated in church, with all its straight lines and sharp corners, I felt cut off from me and yearned to be outdoors. What's it going to be like, I wondered, when I go back to New York and have to work inside all day, every day?

Slipping past the greeters at the door, I returned to the office of the inn and called Mom. She answered after several rings and explained that she was on her way out to the garden. I told her about my week and forced stay in Mack's Inn. Now it didn't seem so bad. I needed the break and didn't even know it.

I asked how she was doing. My sister, Amy, had returned to Florida, and Mom was alone for the first time since Dad's passing, six weeks earlier.

"Fine," she said.

I waited for her to continue, encouraging her with my silence.

Finally, she said, "I don't mean to sound ungrateful, Jennifer, but what I have the most trouble with is all the people who want to help. The men from the VFW take turns stopping by each morning, and the women from the church are doing the same. Everyone is so thoughtful, and I do appreciate their kindness, but I just want some time alone." She paused, searching for the right words. "Jen, now that your father's gone, I don't want to hear from others what I should be doing. I want to know who *I* am. I want to know what *I* want."

I was thrilled for her. After almost forty-five years of giving and serving and caring for others, she was finally free to do exactly as she liked, and, more importantly, she had the courage to want to do it.

"Go for it, Mom. That is so cool that you want that. Maybe you could tell people, 'Thanks, but no thanks.'"

"Well, I would hate to do that, but I may have to," she said resolutely.

A comfortable silence fell between us, strangely reminding me of the hours I had stood at her side in the receiving line at Dad's wake. "You know, Mom, I kind of feel the same way. Without Greg here I'm finally starting to ask who I am and what I want. I didn't even realize how I don't think of these things when he's around. It's like he fills up the whole movie screen, and I can't even see myself in the picture.

"Why is it we can only think about *us* when they're gone?" I ended.

"I don't know, dear, I don't know," she said gently.

In truth, my mother and I were probably more prepared to be without our husbands than we realized. We followed two generations of women who lived without men. My maternal grandmother, Frances Flugge, the same one who worked in the Navy shipyards, had divorced before my mother was a year old. Meanwhile, her mother, Augusta Wagner Flugge, had packed her husband's suitcase and left it outside the door, indicating he could live elsewhere (at least that's how I heard the story). In any event, my grandmother, great-grandmother, and great-great-aunt Lena Wagner, raised my mother without a husband between the three of them.

I love to recall the strength and independence of these women. Their courage and resolve to be true to themselves, during an era when women were expected to stay married at all costs, strengthened my conviction to finish this hike on my own. Though what I was doing was frivolous compared to their struggles for survival, I was proud to join their ranks.

Before hanging up, I invited her to join us for our end-of-hike celebration in Chama, New Mexico. Greg planned to fly out for the last four days, and we were asking all our friends and family to meet us in Chama. Other than my sister, Linda, I hadn't heard from anyone who planned on coming.

She sounded hesitant, uncertain if her finances would be straightened out by then. Mostly she was worried about the long drive from Indiana to New Mexico, something she had never done alone in her forty-six years of marriage. I was disappointed but understood.

At the close of our conversation I walked across the bridge for lunch: baked chicken, mashed potatoes and gravy, corn on the cob and iced tea. Wow! After returning to my cabin I ate a Snickers bar and popcorn — until I was so full it hurt. An hour later I ate two Pop-Tarts. I couldn't stop myself.

My appetite was ferocious even when I was full. I had lost ten pounds since starting the hike and was now 125 pounds. This was the lightest I had been since my sophomore year of high school. Yet, I wasn't willing to carry more food while on the trail. It was simply too heavy. On the other hand, my constant eating in town wasn't fun anymore, either; it was disgusting and disturbing to see what little control I had over my compulsion to eat. I had to wonder if this was how starving people felt. If so, I could begin to appreciate the dangerous lengths to which they would go to feed themselves.

When I returned to my cabin I waxed my boots, replaced the worn straps of my gaiters and filled in a few post cards. Chores accomplished, I got out my journal and wrote. Hours later I dropped the pen from my cramped hand and stretched my back. Surprised to find it growing dark, I made a fresh cup of hot chocolate and slowly read what I had written. My last entry was a quote from P. K. Price, a contributing author in a book Luke had sent to me, titled, *Solo*. The small paperback was an inspiring collection of essays written by women alone in the outdoors.

In "Navigational Information for Solo Flights in the Desert," she wrote:

> Avoid going home at all costs. It is too dangerous. Stay out there. Stay with the desert wherever you go. Even if you must remove your body and cart it back to the city.

I felt the truth of her words, and it scared me. I had only six weeks left on the hike and didn't want it to end. Would I be able to stay with the trail, even after carting my body back to New York?

Chapter 12

Old Faithful Snack Bar
Mack's Inn, ID south
to Yellowstone National Park, WY

During the fall of 1988, fire swept across the Madison Plateau; it destroyed large sections of Yellowstone National Park, as well as surrounding regions. Hours after leaving Mack's Inn, I entered the western edge of this burned-out forest. Blackened trees stood in patches while tall grass and wildflowers dominated the landscape.

Late in the afternoon I searched for Latham Spring, the only known water source in thirteen miles. Walking along the upper rim of a gully, I scanned its depths for signs of water: a pool, a stream, moisture, darkened sand, heavier than usual vegetation. Nothing.

I slid down the sandy bank and began searching. Fallen trees blocked my path as I wove my way past clumps of sage and cacti. Reaching the end without success, I turned to face the setting sun and walked back up the gully.

I shielded my eyes from the blinding rays and stepped over a fallen tree. Pain stabbed through my knee. The stub of a branch was embedded in the tissue beneath my kneecap.

I don't have time for this, I thought, and reached to pull it out.

It didn't budge. I pulled again. Still it didn't move. I wondered if it might really be that deep or if I was unconsciously loosening my grip, afraid of the pain. I shut my eyes as I gripped the branch with both hands and pulled as hard as I could.

It popped out and blood streamed down my leg, turning my sock a deep crimson. I took off my pack, smeared antibiotic cream on a Band-Aid and stuck it to my bloody knee. It fell to the ground, soaked through.

I picked it up and pressed it to the wound, hoping to stem the flow of blood. A few minutes passed, and I pulled it aside to peer at the wound. The bleeding was slowing down. Using spit and my bandana, I cleaned the area around the cut and put on a clean Band-Aid. It stuck. Sighing with relief, I threw on my pack and resumed my search for water.

When I reached the end of the gully, I gave up on finding Latham Spring and climbed out. Backtracking a mile, I returned to a section of the dirt road where rolling banks had been cut into its surface. They looked like giant speed bumps. They were either part of the firefight, or they had a very serious speeding problem in the area. My little joke seemed hilariously funny, and I laughed out loud as I took off my pack.

A small mud puddle lay in a depression between two of these mounds. It was two feet by three feet and held very muddy water. Earlier I had noticed it on my search for the spring but hadn't considered using it to cook dinner; I assumed I would find water in less than a mile. But now I was back and grateful to have it.

In my journal I wrote:

This is my first injury of the trip. It's scary to see how quickly and easily my skin can be punctured. It's unsettling. It can happen with the slightest wrong step, and, once done, there's no taking it back.

Two days passed, and there I was, leaving Madison Plateau and descending into the Biscuit Basin region of the Yellowstone National

Park. The trail lost its backcountry vagueness and became broad and smooth, trodden by a fraction of the park's millions of visitors. Knowing that tourists rarely ventured more than a mile or two into the backcountry, I knew I was close. Like a horse headed back to the barn, I quickened my pace.

Steam seeped from the ground on both sides of the trail, and I came upon a small pool of aquamarine water. The pungent odor of sulfur filled my nostrils as I slowed to investigate. The plant life had given the pool a wide berth, wary of its scorching presence.

I leaned closer to study the colorful display and realized the pool might extend under the trail. The weight of my body could collapse it, spilling me into the boiling water. I stepped back. A shiver ran up my spine; it was as though an evil force had intended me harm. Yet, I knew that wasn't true. Nature was just nature, sometimes beautiful and glorious, other times dangerous and threatening.

Within a few minutes the sparkling sunlight and gently rising steam calmed me, and I felt once again like I had stepped into a magical, sacred place, one filled with the ethereal bodies of angels. I tried to imagine what it was like for early settlers or Native Americans to discover this valley. I wondered if they, too, felt compelled to pray.

The trail ended at the edge of a raised wooden boardwalk. A dozen tourists walked in broad circles, gazing at bubbling pools and blue sapphire geysers. I hadn't seen a person in three days, and it took me a while to become accustomed to this sudden crowd. Though some people glanced my way, no one spoke to me, not even a mumbled hello. How strange, I thought.

They seemed isolated in their bright clothing and flashing cameras — isolated from one another as well as from the park they were visiting. I questioned whether they could feel the power of nature standing on a boardwalk with a secure railing. Hadn't it been the moment I realized I could get burned at the trailside pool that I came to respect it? When I was vulnerable to the scorching water, nature was in charge, not me.

If I didn't want to get hurt, I had to play by nature's rules, not mine. But that was rarely the case on the boardwalk.

These small geysers had been captured within its wooden structure, tamed and civilized to prevent the risk of danger to visitors. No wonder everyone looked so bored. They had no real experience for what they witnessed. It made me wonder. How can we be good stewards of Earth when so few of us have direct experience and respect for its nature?

I did understand that many of these tourists came here with the sincere desire to experience Yellowstone. I had — twelve years earlier. My brother, Joe, and I drove from Indiana, eager for an adventure. During our two day stay, we followed a herd of tourists on a well-worn trail to see the Yellowstone River at Canyon Village then went on a horse ride that was so slow one man fell asleep and slid off his mount. We walked on the boardwalks and sat in the bleachers when Old Faithful shot into the air. We did it all, we thought, and left disappointed.

The scenery had been beautiful, but we were too protected to have an adventure, too corralled to make any discoveries. Now I was just as eager to get back to the *real* Yellowstone National Park, the one that stretched for hundreds of square miles beyond the ken of most of its visitors — the backcountry. But first I had a date with the Old Faithful Snack Bar.

After a double bacon cheeseburger, fries and three sodas, I purchased an ice cream and walked outside. Two backpackers were seated at a picnic table. I joined them.

"Do you guys know where the trailhead is?" I asked to break the ice.

The man closest to me swiveled on his bench and squinted across the parking lot. "Should be over there somewhere," he said and pointed.

I looked and saw no indication of a trail. I didn't really mind; I was sure to find it. I just wanted to talk to someone I could relate to. "So, where you headed?" I asked.

In front of Sapphire Pool in Biscuit Basin of the Yellowstone National Park, Wyoming. (Photo: unknown tourist)

"Back to Iowa. We've been out here for five days and just finished a loop around Yellowstone Lake. How 'bout you?"

"South of here, Shoshone, Lewis, Heart lakes, out that way." I paused before saying more, nervous about looking like I was bragging, but they seemed to be interested. "Actually, I'm hiking all the way to New Mexico, doing the Continental Divide."

Their faces lit up, and we spent the next ten minutes discussing routes, gear, mileage and food. I so enjoyed talking to them that I failed to notice the park ranger coming up the sidewalk.

"Hey, there's a ranger," Tom interrupted, "I bet he'll know where the trailhead is." Before I could stop him, Tom waved him over to our table.

He was easily 6 feet 3 inches and wore the green slacks and hat of the National Park Service. He smiled as he approached us.

"Say, can you tell us where the southbound trailhead is?" Tom asked. "Jen's looking for it." He gestured toward me.

I nodded hello and got ready to leave.

"Sure," he said. "If you'll just step over here, you'll be able to see it."

I said goodbye and followed the ranger to the edge of the road. He pointed out the trailhead and then turned toward me. I was fearful he might ask to see my backcountry permit. In the preceding month I had called Yellowstone several times to change the dates of my permit to match my estimate of when I would arrive. They had readily accommodated me and mailed a new permit. In spite of that, I was still two days early; I no longer had time to wait for a change. I decided to hike through anyway.

I risked being caught and escorted to the southern entrance of the park. From there I would have to hike a hundred miles through the Bridger-Teton National Forest to get back to the CDT — without a map. I was surprised the ranger hadn't already asked to see my permit. In Glacier National Park they checked them as routinely as a state trooper asking for your driver's license.

I thanked him for the directions and headed across the parking lot. Afraid he might realize his mistake and call me back, I cut behind the first RV I saw.

That night I sat on my bivy sack, wearing my fleece sweater and hat. Though it wouldn't be September for another week, the temperature dropped into the forties in the evenings. Autumn was coming with winter not far behind.

Peering at my map in the growing dusk, I swore softly. I had forgotten to call the Cowboy Village Resort at Togwotee and change my reservation. It was 89 miles to Togwotee Pass, and I was scheduled to arrive in three days. I doubted I could hike 30 miles per day through Yellowstone and the Bridger-Teton National Forest. Disappointed, I hoped they had a room open on the thirtieth. If not, I would probably keep hiking without a break. The resort lodge stood alone in the pass; the nearest town was twenty miles west. Then it occurred to me — maybe I *could* hike it in three days.

Excited by the challenge, I tried to figure out if I had a chance of doing that. I had only once backpacked more than thirty miles in a day. That was in the Red Desert, where it was flat, and we followed straight roads most of the time. But three months had passed, and I was a stronger hiker now. I searched the map for clues on the terrain ahead and ultimately decided I would only know if I tried.

I woke just as the sky was beginning to lighten and was soon on the trail headed south. By noon I had a quick swim in Shoshone Lake, and for the next several hours I followed the Shoshone Lake Trail as it wound to the southeast.

Numerous streams crossed its path, most of which were easily forded. But in the late afternoon I came upon a broad tributary feeding into Lewis Lake. It had eaten into the bank on which I stood, placing me about five feet above the water.

A man stood on the far bank. He looked to be Native American. He was carrying a fishing rod in one hand, a tackle box in the other and was about to cross the stream. Seeing me, he stepped back to let me go first.

I gestured for him to go ahead, grateful for the break.

He insisted. Looking clean and strong, he set down his fishing gear and extended his arm to help me across. I slid down the bank, stepped off a boulder and used my trekking poles to pole-vault over the stream — something I had done hundreds of times. He dropped his arm. Embarrassed at my rudeness in not letting him help, I hesitated before charging on down the trail.

"Any luck?" I asked and nodded to his rod.

"Just getting started," he said softly.

His face and arms were tanned, and I picked up his scent — clean and comforting.

"Nice job crossing the stream," he said. He seemed in no hurry to move on.

Suddenly, neither was I. "Yeah, well, these help a lot." I held up my poles. "Want to try them?"

He shook his head no and glanced down at his fishing gear.

"Do you fish here often?" I asked, ignoring the throbbing of my feet and the urgency to keep hiking.

"Yeah, I like to come here after work and catch a few trout." He gazed past me at the flowing river. The strong contour of his cheekbones swept to a point just beneath his mouth — almost as soft and delicate as a woman's. "It's real nice out here. Peaceful." He shifted his gaze back to me.

Caught staring, my face grew hot, and I turned to go.

"You'll see my truck parked at the road. It's the blue Ford," he added quietly before I left.

"I'll be sure to say hi to it," I told him with a smile.

A quiet chuckle reached my ears as I moved to leave. He had enjoyed my small joke.

Winding my way through the woods, I couldn't help but think of him. He seemed so quiet and in tune with nature . . . I imagined staying back there, taking off my pack, watching him bait and cast his rod. I pictured sitting on the bank with nothing to do but enjoy the stillness of the late afternoon, broken only by our occasional talk. Later we would work our way through the dark to his blue Ford and drive to his trailer home. In my fantasy he fried the fish while I took a shower. Afterward, he wrapped his arms around me as we lay together in his bed. We didn't talk or make love, just held each other until we drifted off to sleep.

By the time I reached his truck in the parking lot, I had been living with him for months and our first child was due. Should I leave a note? I wondered.

"And say what?" I asked myself sternly as the fantasy receded.

"I'm a married woman — and I'm just plain ol' lonely," was the answer.

I hiked on past his blue Ford and hurried off along the southeast trail.

During the next hour, the wind picked up enough to cause the lodgepole forest to sway. The charred trunks told of the fire that had swept over this hilltop, and I could clearly see Heart Lake through the barren forest, my intended campsite on its far shore.

A distant view of Heart Lake, my last campsite in Yellowstone National Park, Wyoming. (Photo: Jennifer Hanson)

Limbs scraped and cracked as I continued down the path, and I eyed the trees above me, nervous that one might fall. Just the day before I saw an eighty-foot lodgepole pine crash to the ground for no apparent reason. It had landed less than fifteen feet from my trail, and it wasn't even windy.

Should I turn back? I slowed as I considered. A falling tree could kill me in seconds, and these looked ready to drop. I could see the lake from where I stood. It couldn't be more than a mile or so. If I go back, I'll have to backtrack at least a mile to find water and camp.

I didn't want to be another stupid casualty in a national park; but, on the other hand, I hated the idea that I might be spooking myself into turning back. So, I silently said the Prayer for Protection, and continued forward, my chest tight with fear.

The windy forest dominated my thoughts, and I couldn't stop picturing a tree falling on me. I repeated the Prayer for Protection aloud:

"The Light of God surrounds Us,
"The Love of God enfolds Us,
"The Power of God protects Us,
"and the Presence of God watches over Us,
"Where ever we are God is! And all is well!
"Amen."

When I reached its end I became silent, and the swaying pines flooded my senses. I said the prayer again, louder, and felt a little safer.

After repeating it six or seven times, it occurred to me to sing the prayer, though I had never heard it sung before. I picked a simple melody and tried out the first line. It was flat and weak but infinitely more interesting than saying it. I found a different tune and tried again.

This new melody seemed right. I worked with each line until the words fit the music, and I had a smooth flowing hymn. Pleased with my creation, I sang it repeatedly, my fears largely forgotten. I began modifying my prayer, changing God to Goddess and adding arm gestures to act it out as well as sing it. By the time I left the forest and began my descent to Heart Lake, I felt utterly safe and looked after. Over the weeks to come, I would often sing my prayer to protect myself from all kinds of dangers, real and imagined.

The morning after my time of singing and prayer, I followed the Snake River southeast until I reached a boggy meadow with a wooden post. The sign facing me read, "Entering the Bridger-Teton National Forest." Behind it was, "Entering the Yellowstone National Park."

After crossing Mink Creek, my trail climbed steeply to the Continental Divide. From its rocky ridge I enjoyed views of the snow-capped Grand Tetons — forty miles to the southwest. Soda Mountain and Younts Peak were straight ahead; behind me was the Absaroka Range. It amazed me that with my own two feet I could walk up, over and around these giants.

The day went well. By five o'clock in the afternoon, I covered twenty-six miles. Adding that to the thirty-one miles I hiked the day before brought my total to fifty-seven miles, thirty-two short of Togwotee.

My trail wrapped around the base of a small rise where a large pine tree caught my attention. It was perched at the edge of a flat shoulder of the hill and had a commanding view of the stream-fed meadow. That would be a beautiful place to camp, I mused. Good enough for an ad in *Backpacker* magazine. But I had three hours of daylight and four miles to go; I couldn't stop — unless there is no water ahead, I thought. I pulled out my map to check.

There was plenty of water for camping all along the trail. My route would cross the valley, climb 700 feet and enter a meadow similar to this one — stream and all. I could be there in two hours with plenty of daylight left to set up camp. I visualized the distant meadow to entice me to get started. It didn't work.

Instead, I climbed the bank and stood at the base of a tree. The views were spectacular. A rainbow of wildflowers grew along the creek bed, and a forest of lodgepole pines blanketed the surrounding hillsides. If I camp now, I thought, I would have time to write a letter to my friend, Melany Kahn. And write in my journal, as well. I stared down into the gurgling stream, tempted.

Forget it, I thought. If I don't hike these four miles tonight, then I'll never make it to Togwotee tomorrow. Even if I did, I would get there so late the restaurant would be closed.

I looked around the meadow and was spellbound by its beauty and peacefulness. Couldn't I stop early for once, I wondered, even without a good reason? This is supposed to be some sort of vacation, isn't it?

Screw it, I thought, and decided to camp. I dropped my pack to the ground and scowled at it. I was disappointed I was quitting early, giving up on my goal of making ninety miles in three days.

I pulled my water bottle out of its pouch and went to fill it. The stream was ice-cold; water splashed over my hand as I held the bottle in place. I didn't move it, strangely satisfied with its aching. It was like I was being punished for quitting early. The bottle filled, and still I held it under the water. My skin turned blue, and the bones of my hand felt like they were being crushed. A minute passed, then two. I jerked the bottle out of the water, awed and a little frightened by what I was doing.

Walking back to my camping spot, I told myself it really didn't matter. If I wanted to keep hiking, I could, and if I wanted to stop, that was all right too. In the end these few miles weren't going to make that much of a difference.

As I sat on the ground with the stove simmering between my outstretched legs, I remembered something Greg had told me on our last day together.

"Jen," he had said as he held both my hands in our hotel room, "I know how you are, Babe, and I want you to listen to me. This is important." He paused, waiting for me to nod, to look him in the eye.

"When you're out there alone, Jen, don't push yourself too hard." I started to shrug off his words, but he interrupted me. "I've seen you, Babe, you push and push and push, and without me there to tease you and get you to lighten up, I'm afraid you'll push until you break."

Steam billowed from the pot, untended. Greg was right, I thought, and I began to cry. "I have to lighten up," I cautioned myself and stared blankly at the stove. Its roar drowned out the melody of nearby frogs and crickets. I turned the stove off and wiped the tears from my face.

When the pot cooled, I gently warmed my hands on its sides.

Chapter 13

Lonely
Yellowstone National Park south to Wind River Range, WY

I threw a stick into Two Ocean Creek and waited to see which way it would go. Fifteen feet downstream the brook split at the base of a pine tree. On its trunk was a wooden sign that read, "Atlantic Ocean — 3,488 miles," beside an arrow pointing to the left and "Pacific Ocean — 1,353 miles," next to an arrow pointing to the right. I was on Two Ocean Plateau in the Bridger-Teton National Forest, hoping my twig would go west.

It caught in an eddy and went nowhere. I sank to my haunches, waiting. The authors of the book, *Where the Waters Divide,* had performed this same ritual when they hiked past here a few years earlier. They must have been standing right here, I thought, as I looked around at the small clearing on the bank of the creek. Feeling less alone, I watched as my twig began to spiral in widening arcs. It broke free of the eddy, headed downstream, skimmed across a wide pool and plopped into the Atlantic Creek.

Bummer, I thought.

My twig was headed east, away from the mountains, across the Great Plains and toward the Atlantic Ocean, just as I would when I finished the trail. I sighed and stood up. I felt more at home in these mountains than I had anywhere in my life, and I didn't want to leave.

Two Ocean Creek in northern Wyoming splits along the Continental Divide, a portion flowing toward the Atlantic Ocean, the rest to the Pacific Ocean. (Photo: Jennifer Hanson)

A half-hour later I emerged from the tree line and saw horse packers across the mile-wide valley: four riders with a couple of spare mules trailing dust behind them. Wary as a fox, I melted into the shade of the trees. I had no particular reason to be cautious; it wasn't like I was on private land or hiking without a permit. But, like the animals in the forest, my instinct was to be wary.

They seemed to be following a trail that ran perpendicular to my own. As they came closer, I could clearly make out the riders, and two of them were children. I relaxed. It was a family. Once they were ahead of me I left the trees and headed across the field.

I didn't know how fast a horse would walk with a rider and full saddlebags, but I wasn't surprised that they pulled ahead. By the time their trail turned up the next hill, I figured that was the last I would see of my horse-packing family. Not so.

Two hours later I climbed the low ridge and came upon two boys shrieking and splashing under a waterfall. When they saw me on the trail the oldest crossed his arms in front of his undershorts and spun around. When he looked over his shoulder, I waved and headed on.

Their parents weren't much farther; I stopped to talk as Lois and Bill Bass unpacked their mules and prepared lunch. They looked as comfortable horse-packing as most families would be on a picnic lunch. Lois spread peanut butter and jelly while Bill wrestled the harness off one of his mules.

"See?" He held the strap in front of me.

"Huh?" I asked, uncertain of what I was looking at.

"Chewed through. Damn mules," Bill muttered, then tossed it on top of the saddlebags. "Headed to Togwotee, are you? Well, do you know of the cut-off?"

I shook my head no. "Is it on the map?"

"I doubt it, but I could point it out for you."

While I retrieved my map, Lois asked, "You've really been hiking for five months?"

"Nearly," I said, pleased that she asked. I answered her questions about my food, gear and what it was like to hike alone. She seemed impressed by my journey, and though she asked about my safety, she didn't exude the overwhelming concern that most women had. It was a welcome change.

Her husband, Bill, was a forest ranger for the Bridger-Teton National Forest. They had lived just outside its borders for six years. Within a month they would be transferred to Pueblo, Colorado. This weekend outing was their way of saying goodbye to the forests and mountains they called home.

"Why don't you stay for lunch?" she asked, her brown eyes imploring. "We have plenty."

"Oh, no," I blurted, suddenly nervous. "I really got to get going —

got a lot of miles to cover today."

She seemed disappointed, but Bill took his cue and pointed out the cut-off trail to Togwotee. I was embarrassed by my blunt refusal of lunch, and in my anxiety to leave, I missed much of what he was saying.

Cursing myself as I hiked up the hill, I couldn't understand why I made such a big deal out of a simple invitation to lunch. I would have loved to stay and eat with them. But as I replayed her invitation in my mind, I knew I was afraid. Afraid she would see how lonely I was.

Two hours later I was putting on my boots after lunch when the Bass family rode by on their horses. I waved and smiled, my embarrassment forgotten in the joy of seeing familiar faces. As the older boy passed, I teased, "Don't worry, I didn't see anything."

He blushed and looked away.

His mother smiled.

I hurried to tie my boots and followed them on the trail. Entering a wide meadow, I jumped over a stream, then paused to let them gain distance on me. I certainly didn't want to become a nuisance by spooking their mules. When they were a half-mile ahead I resumed hiking. As they approached the tree line I sped up, not wanting to lose them again.

Passing through the wooded hillside, I caught glimpses of them as they topped a small rise, and later I followed them through another clearing.

Throughout the long afternoon, the Bass family not once turned to wave or otherwise indicate they were aware of my following them. I didn't know if they were trying to ditch me, had forgotten I was there or intentionally went slower so I could keep up. In any event, I enjoyed being a part of their group and was content to tag along like a lost puppy.

I was surprised then, when, around six in the evening, Bill turned his horse and hollered back to me. "Turn-off's just ahead. I'll show you."

I waved my arm in acknowledgement.

At the next rise I found the Bass family huddled together in the chilly evening. They were still mounted and waiting for me to catch up. Lois smiled wearily.

Bill climbed off his horse. "This way," he said and led his mount into the brush.

We came to a small bluff overlooking the confluence of the Soda and Buffalo Rivers. An open marsh stretched over a mile across and several miles in each direction. On the far side was a steep hill where Bill said I would find a trail to the lodge at Togwotee Pass. Finished, he remounted, then spun around to face me and asked if I needed any water.

I didn't.

"Well, why don't you take this?" Bill said. "It's just melting in my saddlebag anyway." He dug a full size Snickers bar from a pouch and held it out for me.

My eyes smarted with sudden tears. I thanked him and took the candy bar.

With that, he nodded once and was gone.

Though I didn't make it all the way to Togwotee Mountain Lodge that night, they easily transferred my reservation, and the next afternoon I gratefully stepped into a steaming hot shower and heard the phone ring. I couldn't think of anyone who knew I was there, so I stayed in the shower. Later, I found out that it was Bill and Lois, calling to make sure I had made it all right.

When I entered the lodge restaurant for dinner I glanced at a stack of newspapers and was shocked by the headline. For the first time since beginning the hike, I bought a paper.

It was August 31, 1997, and Princess Diana had died in a car accident.

Stunned and saddened, I remembered the excitement I felt years before when I first read of her pending marriage with Prince Charles. Not having a royal family of our own, I think I did as many other Americans and adopted England's.

I loved to see their faces smiling out at me as I stood in the checkout line of the grocery store and later delighted in watching Prince William and Prince Henry grow up. Somehow the world had seemed a better place with the royal family in it. Now she was gone.

The morning after the sad news, I climbed a cow path to the Divide, and by noon I crossed a small hill overlooking Warm Spring Creek. A flock of sparrows took sudden flight, and a coyote looked up at me, startled. He stood on the near side of the valley, and though he was nearly a quarter of a mile away, I could clearly make out his bushy tail and tall ears.

I froze, and we stared at one another for several long seconds, then he dashed through the thick brush that surrounded the creek. With a commanding view of the valley, I was able to track his progress through the undergrowth. I saw the bushes shake and heard him splash across the stream. Climbing the far bank, he reached the base of the distant slope and stopped. In plain view, he watched me.

It occurred to me that he might be trying to divert my attention from elsewhere, perhaps a nearby den. In any event, it worked. He had my undivided attention until I grew bored with the standoff.

I imagined I was a mountain man from the 1800s, and I drew my hiking pole level with my shoulder. I sighted the coyote over its tip. Squinting one eye, I adjusted for wind and distance, and slowly pulled the trigger.

"Click," I whispered, and he bolted.

Startled and feeling guilty, I watched him disappear into the spruce-fir forest. Had he perceived my fantasy intention from so far away? He must have, I concluded, and regretted my violent gesture.

I stopped at the edge of the creek for lunch, its grassy banks perfect for my daily chore of drying my bivy sack, pad and sleeping bag. While I ate my typical mid-day meal of nuts, jerky, and crackers, I pulled out a large booklet, *History of Wyoming,* and read tales of Union Pass during the mid-1800s. I was scheduled to hike there the next day and was intrigued by the stories of the trappers and traders who had once roamed the Wind River Range.

Loud barking interrupted my reading. I scanned the far hillside, but was unable to find the coyote. I was certain it was the same animal, and he didn't sound happy that I was still at his creek.

"Hey, coyote," I yelled, mostly for fun. "Don't worry. I'm not staying. I'll be gone in fifteen minutes." He immediately stopped barking, though I felt him watching me until I left the valley.

The trail I followed grew wider and eventually became a jeep road, winding through some of the most rolling country I had passed. I topped a small hill and stopped. Beneath me, not more than thirty yards away, smack in the middle of my trail, was a single bull. His horns seemed to spread as wide as he was long; his coat was pure black. My stomach tightened. I considered going around but discarded the idea. It would take too long.

"Go on," I shouted, dismissing him with a wave of my arm. "Go lay down," I said as though I were commanding my dogs, while my insides turned to jelly. He looked away, hesitant. I shouted again, more boldly now. He took a few steps into the field. "That's right. Go on," I shouted, walking forward, still waving my arm and poles. He ambled away, then snorting, trotted off on his thin legs.

I couldn't believe it. I had just told a bull to go away, and he did. Still quivering inside, I walked where he had stood and continued on my way — laughing.

Hours later, I was approaching Gunsight Pass, and two things happened. The jeep road split, and it started to rain. The pass was straight ahead in little over a mile, a distance I usually covered in eighteen minutes. In this case it took two hours. It would have been longer, but I finally abandoned all hopes of finding the trail and bushwhacked straight to it. Sweaty, buggy, and bleeding, I arrived at Gunsight Pass, took off my pack and sat down.

Before me was the sweep of the Green River Valley, the western gateway to the Wind River Range. The scene was stunning. Fierce storm clouds blanketed the mountains while shafts of sunlight gleamed off the white cliffs surrounding the Green River Lakes.

It's like looking into a human soul, I thought, filled with mysterious, exciting depths that are sometimes shrouded in a dark mood. I laughed aloud, amused with my poetic description as I stood up, put on my pack and hustled along.

It was a quick descent on the steep eastern slope. At the base I passed mixed herds of cattle and elk in the trees, then headed due south to the Green River, a half-mile away. I was surprised by how wide the Green River was and searched the map for a bridge. The nearest was at the campground, four miles east.

A car drove down a gravel road across the river; dust stretched behind it like the bushy tail of a squirrel. It'll probably be in the campground in less than fifteen minutes, I thought, and resisted the urge to sit down. I knew from experience that the four mile bushwhack to the campground bridge could take two to three hours of frustrating, exhausting hiking. But if I were on that road, I thought, I could be there in a little over an hour — easy.

I studied the river closely. It was about seventy feet wide, shallow and muddy, with a fence stretched from one bank to the other. Could I wade across? No, probably not. My response bothered me, since I had read that my ability to survive in the outdoors could be predicted by my knee jerk response to a seemingly impossible situation. If you thought you could do it, you could. If you doubted yourself, you didn't have what it took.

I stared at the river, wondering why I thought I couldn't cross. Very good reasons came to mind: it was too deep, too fast, too cold and too wide. Bottom line, it wasn't safe. But maybe it's not too deep.

I hiked to the river and stood at its edge. The current was faster than I had suspected, yet the water seemed shallower. I considered starting across, and if it got too deep, turning back. Down river was as wide, muddy and featureless as where I stood. Even if I were swept off my feet, I could just swim out.

I decided to go for it. Excited, I took off my boots and moved my GPS and camera to the hood of the pack. Standard backpacking safety called for me to undo my hip belt before crossing, reducing the risk of being pulled underwater by my gear. But I had always questioned how many unbuckled packs caused hikers to lose their balance in the first place. I tightened my hip belt and stepped into the water.

It was cold — very cold. The current swirled around my bare calves and thighs while my flip-flops sank into the muddy bottom. Never mind. I started across.

The water rose quickly, and within ten feet it was soaking my running shorts. I decided to turn back.

Knew I couldn't make it, I thought, angry that I had doubted myself in the first place, jinxing my chances of success. I began my wide careful turn. In doing so I came closer to the rancher's fence and discovered that the river was more shallow there. By staying close to the barbed wire I might be able to continue. Thrilled, I kept going.

When I was only fifteen feet from the far bank, the bottom of the river changed. Like quicksand, there seemed to be nothing solid to push off from. One foot sunk deep into the muck while I struggled to pull the other out, the hard plastic thong digging into the flesh of my toes.

At some point during this painful process, I wondered if I should turn back. but I decided to give it another few minutes and see what happened. To my relief, it got easier. I soon reached the edge of the water and pulled myself onto the grassy bank.

I made it, I thought, delighted with myself. Smiling, I stretched back on the grass and kicked my bare feet in the air. The sun warmed them, and for a few minutes I basked in victory. I wondered how many times I had walked away from what I wanted — simply because I didn't think I could do it. Now I knew differently. I could always try. And who knows, maybe trying is enough!

Chapter 14

Race the Coming Winter
Wind River Range, WY
south to South Pass, WY

A thick fog blanketed the Green River Lake Campground and its valley the next morning. I was accustomed to seeing for miles in this arid land, and my limited view was disorienting. As I hiked across the canyon floor east of the campground it was as though the trail and surrounding cattails were drifting in and out of a dream. The muted echo of a stream confused me as well. At times it sounded far ahead and at other times just under foot or behind me.

I sensed clear skies and a burning sun, yet looking up I saw nothing but swirling fog. The clouds briefly parted, and I glimpsed the faint silhouette of pine trees high on the canyon wall.

At the base of the white rock cliffs the trail turned east. For the next ten miles it slowly gained elevation as it meandered between the aquamarine Green River on my right and the white limestone cliffs on my left. The fog began lifting as the sun burned it away. By ten o'clock all that remained were streaks of cloud suspended between the glowing river below and the sunlit valley above. It was striking, and I stopped often to take pictures.

On one occasion I had just put away my camera when I saw a massive bull moose less than twenty feet away. His rack spanned over five feet, and his tail swished lazily in the forested shade. I froze. He stared at me — motionless. I had heard that bull moose sometimes charge at people. At first I was frightened, but when he didn't move I decided I was safe enough and enjoyed the rare treat of being with a thousand-pound animal in the wild.

I wished I hadn't put my camera away but decided against pulling it out again. I would rather have a few peaceful moments with the moose than a fuzzy picture of his butt as he ran off.

"Thank you, Mr. Moose," I told him softly. "You're magnificent. Do you have a message for me?" I listened to the mountain chickadees, felt the breeze and observed my thoughts but heard no answer. Perhaps one would come later.

He broke eye contact, glanced over his shoulder, then ran into the woods.

I was alone again and filled with wonder.

Recalling the Native tradition of sprinkling tobacco as a gesture of gratitude, I took out my lunch and tore off a piece of jerky. It wasn't sacred tobacco, but it was hard to part with, and I figured that was the point anyway. Holding it in the direction the moose had gone, I thanked him again and left it on the side of the trail.

After leaving the valley I climbed over three boulder strewn passes: Vista, Cubed Rock and Shannon. To the north, lightning streaked above the high peaks of the Divide. Luckily, I was headed east onto a storm-free plateau. At 12,000 feet I was in the high country of the Wind River Range. Rocks, boulders, streams and ponds littered the landscape with only an occasional bush or stubby pine to break the monotonous gray.

As I hiked, the shadow of Stroud Peak fell over me. I had only two miles before camping when I saw a young woman crouched beside a stream at the head of Lower Jean Lake. The knife she wielded sliced the belly of a trout, its entrails spilling onto the stone. She tossed a quick glance and hello to me, then returned to her task. Soon I stood beside her, numb with fatigue.

Anxious to finish the hike before winter, I pushed through the Wind River Range, averaging 22 miles per day. (Photo: Jennifer Hanson)

During short breaks in her work, she told me that she and her boyfriend were on a ten-day hike through the Winds. They had entered north of the Divide and crossed over the high ridge. Now three days into their hike they had eaten more than half of their food and were concerned they would run out.

"We brought the poles to enjoy some fishing, but now we're living off them," she said and laughed.

I liked her. She was rugged, resourceful and light-hearted. I wished she were hiking with me, but alas, I had to continue alone. After lingering for several more minutes, I decided to heed the call of my aching feet, skip those last two miles and set up camp nearby.

The following day I leaned my pack against Big Sandy Lodge and entered the building. To my left opened a large room with three wooden tables set side by side. Sunlight reflected off the polished floors, brightening the cool interior. I walked through the dining area and stuck my head in the kitchen. "Anyone here?"

An older woman stepped into the hallway and wiped her hands on her apron. I explained I had reserved a cabin — but was a day early — and asked if they had any openings. She went to get her husband. He came slowly up the hallway, leaning heavily on his cane. After shaking my hand, he gestured for me to follow him to his office, a converted pantry. I waited in the doorway; there was no room for me inside.

After settling into his chair and arranging his bifocals, he carefully opened a ledger. Leaning forward, he traced each page with his finger as he searched for my reservation. I liked his pace. No quick movements or fast talk here.

Reaching the bottom of the third page, he stopped and turned to me. "Jennifer and Greg Allen?" he asked, looking behind me for Greg.

"It's just me now. Greg won't be coming."

He blinked for several seconds, then returned to his ledger.

"Your reservation is for September 7th." He checked the calendar. "Today's the 6th." Now he waited for an explanation.

"Yeah, I'm a day early. Do you have a cabin available?" I asked, amused that I had to inquire again. What did he want me to do, go back in the woods and wait a day?

"Let's see," he said, and with that he began another search through the book.

We were both startled when his wife yelled from the kitchen, "All filled up! Your reservation is for tomorrow." She came through the door, a wet platter in her hands.

"I know," I told her. "I'm a day early."

"Well, we don't have any room for you tonight; your reservation isn't until the seventh."

"I understand that. Do you have a place where I could camp?"

She shook her head, "No camping allowed."

"All right," I said. "I'll just pick up my mail and get my refund. I already paid full price for the cabin, eighty dollars, right?" I turned to her husband.

He was watching us, finger still pressed to the open page of the ledger.

"Well, you may as well stay for supper," she said, sounding overwhelmed. "I think there's enough for one more." She retrieved my mail and went off to the kitchen. In the end she let me use a spare wrangler's tent, which her twelve-year-old granddaughter was kind enough to equip with a cot, lawn-chair and kerosene lamp.

Perhaps being the most convenient CDT resupply point in the Wind River Range had soured her attitude toward thru-hikers just a tad. Even so, when I overheard the girl being scolded for her thoughtfulness, I wondered just a bit.

Before leaving the next morning I went to square up with the old man. My receipt listed charges for dinner, breakfast, communal shower, holding my mail and using their tent: eighty dollars even. I didn't mind much, considering his wife was such a great cook.

For dinner we had steak, potatoes, corn on the cob and warm brownies. Breakfast was scrambled eggs, pancakes, sausage and orange juice. All of it delicious and "all you can eat" — and I ate plenty. It was a bargain!

While at Big Sandy Lodge, I decided to change my route. I had pushed hard the past ten days and covered 223 miles. It had been tough work. I had originally planned to climb back to the spine of the Wind River Range, but now I considered heading south along the Lander Cutoff to South Pass. Maybe I was getting soft, I don't know, but when my dinner companions that night began describing the northern trail with their arms pumping up and down, I gave it up. I'll have to visit the Cirque of the Towers another time, I told myself.

The dirt road I followed took me through the rolling hills north of the Big Sandy River. After lunch I followed the road up a small rise and saw a herd of sheep below. A man rode his horse behind them while two border collies nipped at their ankles. I realized they were trying to get the herd across the bridge; but, instead of crossing it, they were blocking it. I sat down to wait.

Hundreds of sheep covered the road and spilled into the fields on both sides. There was much bleating and milling about, but only a handful of the bravest ventured onto the wooden planks. The sheepherder and dogs dashed back and forth, hollering and barking. A half-dozen animals splashed into the stream, but the ones on the bridge stayed put. A car arrived from the other direction and waited patiently for the bridge to be cleared.

Finally, the sheepherder dismounted and stormed into the center of the herd, waving his hat and shouting. Animals swirled in every direction. Like a snake, he weaved into the center of the bridge and broke up the clog. The herd spilled over the river and into the meadow on the far side. In what seemed like seconds, the road was clear, the sheep were grazing peacefully and their master was back in his saddle.

As a Christian, I've often heard Jesus likened to a sheepherder, and we as the flock. Until then I always felt comforted by the analogy of being watched after and provided for. Now I had to wonder if unblocking *us* with harmless threats was part of His job.

That night I camped beside a man-made stream that flowed from the only spring on my entire map. The ditch was three inches wide and stretched hundreds of yards across open prairie. After sitting out a late afternoon thunderstorm, I cooked Jiffy-Pop on my stove. It was a treat I had carried since Togwotee Mountain Lodge to celebrate my last night in Wyoming. The prairie was peaceful in the wake of the storm, and I picked up my journal and wrote:

It is so unbelievably quiet that my ears are straining to

hear something. In this huge, open plain I hear naught,
only the occasional flutter of bird wings and my own brain
waves ringing in my ears.

And with that, I climbed into my sleeping bag and fell asleep.

I reached South Pass by noon the next day and gazed up the gravel road that we had followed into the Great Divide Basin in May. So much had changed. Three months ago Dad was still alive, Greg was on the trail, and we had before us almost 2,000 miles through unfamiliar terrain. I had been filled with the excitement and fear of hiking into the unknown.

Now it was different. I knew what it was like to cross the Red Desert, snowshoe through Colorado, camp in grizzly country and navigate along the Bitterroot Range. Though I looked forward to the 400 miles that remained in southern Colorado, I didn't think it held many surprises for me. My big adventure was winding down.

At a roadside parking area I spread out my gear and cooked lunch. Chris and Kathy Luyckx would pick me up in an hour, something arranged months ago by Chris' brother, Luke, back in New York. I looked forward to spending a day with them at their home in Lander, relaxing among their horses, dogs, cats, fish and birds. Who wouldn't feel at home with so many animals around?

The blue flame of my stove fought against the wind. Removing my boots, I set one on each side of it, shielding it. Satisfied, I continued my letter to a friend:

Summer is ending and so is my hike. How can I turn back the
season and start once again? I'm going to miss it.

I gazed across the wind-blown prairie, listening to grasshoppers leaping in the afternoon sun. Steam billowed from the pot, and I turned it off. While eating I watched an elderly couple share lunch at a nearby picnic table.

I continued my letter:

> *I'm also beginning to feel excited about going home. I look forward to having a regular life, driving a car, going to the movies, wearing jeans. It'll be all right.*
> *But I don't think I'll stop missing the trail. Ever.*

By four o'clock the Luyckxs arrived towing their horse trailer. Sitting in the back seat of their Jeep Cherokee, I was distinctly aware of how soft the seat was. Before the hike I wouldn't have given it a thought, but now it seemed an incredible luxury, and in the back seat, no less. We really do spare ourselves so little in the name of comfort.

Red sandstone hills sped past, and the wind tugged at my shirt. Kathy chatted for a while, but the words tumbled out so quickly that I let them flow past without trying to catch them all. She had a pleasant voice, and I enjoyed listening to the cadence of it. I spotted a banana leaned against the emergency brake up front.

Finally I asked, "Can I have that banana?"

I was sure neither of them wanted it — black at the edges, baking in the sun.

"Yes, of course! Oh, I'm so sorry, I wasn't thinking." Kathy handed me the banana as well as two apples. "Here, help yourself. My God, look at you. You must be starved."

I didn't think I looked that bad but was grateful for the fresh fruit.

That night I slept in the guest bedroom of their house. Sinking into the large mattress, I was honored when their cat nudged open the door and curled up beside me. By the time I got up in the morning, they were both at work. I took a long shower, then walked to the grocery store, where I bought two full bags of fruit, nuts, candy and magazines. I wanted to be ready for my twelve-hour bus ride from Shoshone, Wyoming to Denver, Colorado.

The following day Kathy stopped work early, and they drove me to Shoshone. My bus would leave at six that night. In Denver I would stay at my sister's house for another day before her husband, Art, drove me back to the Rockies to begin the fifth and final leg of my hike: Silverthorne, Colorado to Chama, New Mexico.

I boarded the bus and picked an empty seat about halfway back. Sitting next to the window, I waved goodbye to Chris and Kathy. The bus slid from the station. I looked again for a final glimpse of familiar faces but saw only their bumper as the Luyckxs drove out of the parking lot.

Twelve hours later, as the rising sun was streaking through the windows of the Denver terminal, I got off the bus and was hugged by my brother-in-law, Art. He scooped up my pack and put it in his truck, unbothered by the early-hour pick-up. My sister, Linda, greeted us at the door of their home. It was good to see her again. When I called from Lander she asked if I had any special requests.

"Peanut M&Ms, bacon cheeseburgers, potato chips," I started, "and could you invite twenty of your closest friends?" I was only half teasing.

"Are you sure you can't stay another day, Jen?" my sister asked. Her hands were filled with raw hamburger meat. She had invited a couple over for dinner, and we were getting ready for a barbeque. "You just got here this morning and have been running around all day fixing your gear, shopping, packing and fiddling with your maps. You haven't even had time to call Greg, let alone relax."

"Sorry, Linda, got to go tomorrow. Snow is coming."

"Look, kiddo, I'm just trying to help, but you look like dirt — tired, skinny as a toothpick. And where's your husband? Why isn't he out here helping you?"

The sharpness of her voice took me by surprise. I couldn't understand why she would be upset that Greg wasn't here. Then I realized she must be concerned, not believing I was safe on my own. "He's back at work. Besides, what's he going to do to help?"

"He could have been taking care of your gear today so you could sleep. He could drive you to the trail tomorrow. He could be here in Colorado instead of two thousand miles away in New York, should you run into trouble." Linda slapped a hamburger patty on the platter and frowned at me.

My sister is seven years older and had practically raised me. She's just concerned, I reminded myself. "Linda, I'm going to be all right — really. I know I've lost some weight, and I'm a little tired from the bus trip, but I know what I'm doing out there. Greg didn't abandon me. He really is doing much more by going back to work than by standing around here for two months. I call him from every town stop, he has a beeper so I can reach him quickly, he knows where I'm hiking, and if I don't call, he knows what to do."

"I just want you to be safe, kiddo. People die in the Rocky Mountains every year."

I looked down at my bare feet and nodded my head. It was true what she said, and though I resented her believing I needed a man with me to be safe, she deserved an honest response. Linda might be a little old-fashioned, but she is no alarmist. She is a very bright woman, and she had done enough camping and traveling to know what she was talking about.

"I know, Linda, I know." I looked at her and shrugged. "But it doesn't matter. I've got to finish this hike. I'll be as careful as I can, but I can't stop just because Greg isn't with me."

Later I promised that I would call at every town stop and soon regretted it. Feeling the constraint like bars on a cage, I mourned my days of freedom in Wyoming.

Fifth Leg

From Silverthorne, CO
south to Chama, NM

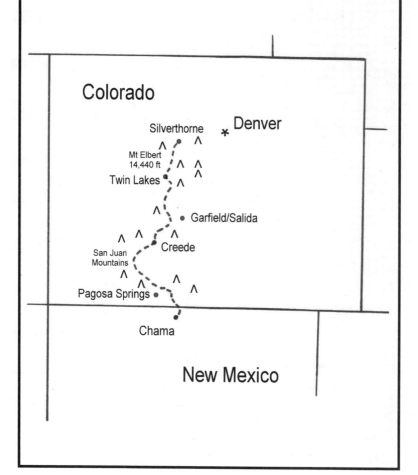

Chapter 15

Finally! Another Thru-hiker
Silverthorne, CO south to San Luis Pass, CO

On September 12th, Linda's husband, Art, dropped me off in Silverthorne at the trailhead. Still bloated from eating my sister's delicious cooking, I wasn't anxious to climb 2,000 feet to the ridge. Feeling lightheaded and sluggish, I listened to thunder from afternoon storm clouds.

Forget it, I decided. I would stick with the lower trail. That would give me a chance to acclimate to the higher elevation and avoid the lightning. The route to Copper Mountain, eight miles south, was straightforward with only one glitch, Interstate Highway 70, which cut right across my route.

Walking along the southbound trail, I enjoyed the soft presence of the golden aspen. Their dried leaves rustled in the breeze, and I was reminded that autumn was almost here — and with it, the promise of snow.

I recalled a conversation I had with Grant Peck, a nature photographer, in the Wind River Range the week before. He emphasized the importance of being prepared for snow in the mountains and told me that one year in late August the Winds had received five feet of snow in two days. Five feet, I thought, in August? I wasn't even carrying snowshoes. How would I hike out of something like that?

The trail was well trodden and easy to follow. It wasn't long before I could hear the steady rush of traffic. I left my path, climbed over a small earthen bank and faced four lanes of racing motorists: I-70.

I stepped back into the tree line and studied my map. It revealed little hope of a road over or under the highway. I considered dashing across. Greg and I had been forced to do that coming into Silverthorne in June, but traffic had been light then. Now it was three in the afternoon and approaching rush hour. Besides, all I needed was for a cop to see me. That would certainly reassure Linda.

I decided to treat it like an un-fordable river and follow its bank until I saw an opportunity to pass. I walked close to the tree line, yet was conspicuously in view of the passing motorists.

I remembered a story I had read of a couple hiking across the United States. One day they were walking on the shoulder of a divided highway when a car struck the woman from behind. She was thrown thirty feet and landed with her pack still on. Miraculously, she suffered only bumps and scrapes, and was backpacking again in a couple of days. After recalling that, I couldn't shake the image of a car hitting me from behind and edged closer to the forest.

I knew walking on the shoulder of an interstate was against the law, but after I hiked 2,000 miles to get here, the law seemed unjust. What gives people the right to build highways, blocking pedestrian traffic, both human and non-human? Who were we to chop up the forest with our impassable roads? Of all the animals I had met, humans were by far the noisiest, most harmful and most arrogant.

I hiked to the first exit and got off. Continuing south, I followed a paved bike trail that paralleled the highway. Bicyclists and roller-bladers glided past me, and though Colorado is famous for its outdoor enthusiasts, I felt self-conscious in my backpack and dirty boots. Acting like I didn't care, I held my poles in one hand and a book in the other. I soon reached the Copper Mountain Ski Resort, hiked across their huge parking lot and found the trailhead for the Colorado Trail.

Two days later at the first sign of dawn I was up and packed in record time. Based on what a group of hikers had told me the night before, there was a CDT thru-hiker only a half-hour ahead of me. I guessed he was camped at Porcupine Creek, a couple of miles up the trail. If so, I had a chance of catching him while he ate breakfast.

I yearned to meet him and wondered if I would finally have the chance to talk to someone who knew the trail like I did. I hurried, imagining him packing his tent, compass slung around his neck. He would probably be glad to meet me and come over to shake my hand.

Coming into the high mountain prairie, I knew the stream was nearby and slowed my pace, suddenly nervous. I worried that he might be weird or a know-it-all, or that he might expect us to hike together.

The trail crossed the stream and ran along side of it for a quarter of a mile. Mist hung two feet above the water, blocked from the sun by St. Kevin Peak. I looked around for a tent or hiker. Nothing.

Just as I decided that he had already left and was beginning to feel disappointed, I spotted him. He sat on the ground in a light blue windbreaker, silently eating a pot of oatmeal. His tent was packed, and aside from his pot and spoon, he looked ready to go. Another ten minutes and I might have missed him.

Though he didn't stand, he seemed surprised and glad to see me. He said, "Hello." His name was Aaron Sheaffer. He was in his early twenties with reddish hair, gray eyes and a scraggly growth of hair that ran under his chin but not on it. As I removed my pack, crouching down to talk with him, he watched silently.

We swapped the usual trail talk: where you started, how far you've come, how far you had to go, what gear you were carrying and whether or not you had seen any other thru-hikers. "Only one," he said.

After a while, I became chilled and wanted to get going. Standing up, I realized he still hadn't finished his breakfast.

"You going to hike or eat all day?" I was trying to sound funny, but it came out rougher than I had intended, and I was embarrassed.

Finally! Another Thru-hiker
Silverthorne, CO south to San Luis Pass, CO

217

Aaron laughed and finished in three scoops. "You don't know how good it was to hear you say that," he told me as I followed him up the trail. "I came out here planning to hike with three other people. I knew two of the guys from the AT last summer. But then Jake decided to bring his girlfriend. Well, she was nice but not much of a hiker. So we were making slow time. One of the things that would drive me crazy was that we would stop for a lunch break and spend over an hour sitting around eating. I was always saying, 'Come on, guys, let's go.' And they would ask, 'What's the rush? We've got all summer!'

"Well, after a month of that, I couldn't take it anymore, and we split up." He paused — seemingly thoughtful. "So, anyway, when you asked if I was going to hike or eat all day, I felt, like, cool! Finally I'm meeting another hiker who thinks like me." He looked up, smiling.

We hiked together throughout the morning, talking off and on. I found myself mechanically following his footsteps, just as I had with Greg. It was strange, but hiking with Aaron made me start missing Greg all over again.

By afternoon we stopped talking and fell back to our own pace and thoughts. Aaron's long legs stretched easily up the inclines, quickly leaving me behind. He didn't slow down or wait; in fact, he didn't even look back to check on me. He must have decided I could do well enough on my own.

Ultimately, I had my turn in the lead, as well, and not because he was being nice. Descending a rocky slope, I caught up with Aaron and passed him. Using my trekking poles, I was able to spill down the mountain on four legs while Aaron had only two.

At the bottom of the hill I pulled off the trail to use the "bathroom" and, while squatting, Aaron passed. He had taken off his wind pants and wore Spandex running shorts along with his blue backpack and wide brimmed cowboy hat. I smiled. It's not often you see a man in the woods wearing a cowboy hat and Spandex shorts.

Though I hurried to catch up, I didn't see him again until he stopped for the night. He had set up his tent in a flat hollow just off the trail. It stood about 300 yards uphill from a small stream and was nestled under the golden branches of an aspen grove.

"Mind if I join you?" I called from the trail.

He waved me over, and I set up my bivy sack, all the while stealing glances to see what he was doing. I secretly hoped he would be impressed with how quickly I set up camp, then chided myself for caring what he thought. After all, he was only a 23-year-old kid.

"Do you know where your friends are now?" I asked while we sat on the ground cooking dinner.

"Last I heard they were in Yellowstone. I doubt they've gotten much farther."

"Geez, they're never going to get through Colorado. They'll be snowed out before they even reach the state."

Aaron shrugged. Finishing his pasta, he dismantled his stove and set it aside. "How's it been hiking without your husband?"

"It's different — kind of hard to describe." I paused, searching for the right words. "It's like without him here, it's just me and the wilderness. Like I'm more a part of the trail and the mountains and animals — less a visitor. Know what I mean?"

Aaron nodded.

"And it wasn't anything he did, I don't think, just that he was there. Another person was there, and I wasn't so in tune, I guess." I shivered in my thin fleece and looked up at the tops of the trees, silhouetted against the darkening sky. "Now that I'm alone, I'm free to totally love it. And I do. I love it. Every single day. I don't care if it's raining or I'm lost or tired, it just feels so good to be out here. I've never been this happy in my life before."

"Yeah, me too." Aaron lifted his head and his eyes searched the

Finally! Another Thru-hiker
Silverthorne, CO south to San Luis Pass, CO

219

sky for early stars. "When I was up in Wyoming I ran into a man who gave me a great compliment. He said I wasn't a tourist or vacationer but a traveler. I liked that, you know. I travel and experience the country. I live in it."

I smiled as night began to fall. I'm a traveler, I thought. It fit. We sat in silence gazing upward, listening to the rustling aspen.

"I have only three weeks left." My voice was hushed, as if confiding. "I wish I could just keep going. Get to the end in Chama and hike all the way to the bottom of South America."

"Yeah, I know what you mean," he responded softly. "You ever hear of those guys who reach Katahdan and turn right around and hike back south to Springer?" he asked, referring to the end and the beginning mountains of the Appalachian Trail.

"Yeah, now I know why they do it."

We sat in the deepening darkness. After a few minutes Aaron stood and said goodnight. I watched the glow of his flashlight through his tent wall as he settled into his sleeping bag. Then it clicked off.

In the morning I sat on the end of my packed bag, double-knotting my bootlaces. As I finished, I looked up to see Aaron just lighting his stove for breakfast. The sun set fire to the golden leaves at the top of the aspen. As it crept down toward us, my impatience grew.

Finally, I stood and hoisted my pack. "I'm going to get a head start, all right?" What was I doing? Asking permission?

"Sure, see you later." He waved his spoon in the air in farewell. I turned and headed south on the Colorado Trail, relieved to be on my own and sorting through my feelings. It was great to have someone to hang out with on the trail, but I missed the freedom of coming and going as I pleased. On the other hand, I noticed Aaron didn't seem to restrict himself because of my presence. He just did as he liked, as though he might've been alone. Perhaps I could do the same.

I hiked up the long trail, lost in thought. Coming to a rocky outcropping overlooking a forested valley, I stopped briefly to catch my breath. A dark haired woman hurrying up the trail startled me.

"Going to Mount Elbert?" she asked.

"Huh, no, hiking the CDT."

"The what?"

"The CDT, Continental Divide Trail — from Canada to Mexico."

"Oh, well, look, you should hike Mount Elbert. The cut-off trail is right ahead." Accustomed to silence and Aaron's slow cadence, I could barely keep up with the rush of her words.

"Sure, all right, good luck," I called out as I watched her scurry away.

Geez, I thought, a day-hiker. When was the last time I saw a day-hiker? And it's only seven-thirty in the morning! What's she doing up so early? I looked back down the trail. No sign of Aaron. I continued up the mountain and reviewed my encounter with the woman. There was something nagging me about what she had said, but I couldn't quite place it.

The well-worn trail followed the ridge and in a half-mile, I saw a side trail to my right. "Mount Elbert — 4.2 miles," it read. Then I remembered. Mount Elbert at 14,433 feet is the highest point in Colorado and the third highest point in the Continental United States. I had always planned to make a detour to hike Mount Elbert, and now I was finally here and had almost missed it! Silently thanking the day-hiker, I scribbled a note to Aaron, stuffed it under a rock in the middle of the trail and headed toward Mount Elbert.

The path wound through forests of juniper, heath and pine, slowly climbing all the way. The trees thinned, and I found myself facing a massive, rocky slope. It climbed high into the clouds, and though the peak was still three miles away, it towered nearly 3,000 feet above me. I could make out most of the trail to the top and a sprinkling of

Finally! Another Thru-hiker
Silverthorne, CO south to San Luis Pass, CO

221

brightly colored dots — people! They were hiking alone or in small groups of two or three, evenly spread about a quarter of a mile apart.

Waiting for my heart rate to subside before pushing on, I ate a candy bar and drank sparingly from my bottle. Water was unlikely at this elevation.

I was glad I still wore my wind pants when I left the shelter of the trees and felt the full brunt of the winds out of the north. Climbing higher, I looked back to see the heavy clouds moving closer. Damn! It had been such a nice morning.

An hour later I stopped and shed my pack. Pulling out my rain jacket, I quickly donned it and tightly zippered it to my chin. I looked down the trail — all the way back to the trees. No sign of Aaron. He must have decided to skip Elbert and head straight to Twin Lakes, Colorado, the next town stop. Though there were no official towns for re-supplying, most of our stops corresponded. This wasn't unusual when you remember there are very few towns convenient to the trail.

I noticed the two guys below me; they were climbing the rock ledge I had crossed only fifteen minutes earlier. Unwilling to be passed by day-hikers, I turned back into the wind and hurried on.

Forty-five minutes later, I climbed onto a rock face, gasping for air. I could see the top. A pile of black-and-rust rocks stood a couple of hundred yards higher than where I was. A few hikers milled around, talking and looking out over the seemingly endless mountain range.

I climbed that last 200 yards and was surprised to find a couple of dozen hikers crouched against a low stone wall shielded from the cold wind. After the long hours of solo climbing, I was unprepared for the sudden onslaught of so many people — voices, colors, gear.

I turned away and let my eyes take in the panorama of the Rocky Mountains. It was as though I might be looking out the window of an airplane. Clouds hung above, beside and below, giving me the impression that I was truly in the sky. I searched out the details of individual peaks: Mt. Massive, Jenkins Mountain, La Plata Peak and many more. I saw avalanche sights, golden aspen groves and the rich shades of evergreen forests. I traced the flow of streams to rivers to lakes and, turning, saw my resupply town wedged between the steep foothills of Mount Elbert and the glistening Twin Lakes. Turning south, the wind slipped beneath my collar and sent a chill between my breasts. It was time to go. But first I wanted to get a picture of myself on the top.

I approached a group of young guys who were laughing and joking. They were shivering in their sweatshirts as they looked out over the view.

"Mind taking our picture?" I shouted to be heard over the wind. One man reached for my camera as I wrapped my arm around another. He good-naturedly leaned close to me and posed for the picture.

"Thanks, my name's Jennifer," I shouted.

"Pete! No problem," he shouted back.

"See you guys at the bottom."

Posing with another hiker at the top of Mount Elbert, 14,433 feet — the highest point in Colorado. (Photo: Unknown hiker)

Finally! Another Thru-hiker
Silverthorne, CO south to San Luis Pass, CO

223

When I reached Twin Lakes I found Aaron seated outside a building, a pile of mail beside him.

"You climbed Elbert, didn't you?" he asked when he saw me.

Grinning, I nodded.

"I missed it. Didn't even realize it was there until my dad asked me on the phone a minute ago. How was it?"

"It was pretty cool — but not that different from a lot of other mountain tops, just more people." I didn't want him to feel disappointed. I pointed to his mail. "Where's the Post Office?"

"Right there," He gestured to the building next door, "In the back of the convenience store. And there's no coin laundry or gas station in town. I already checked."

"Oh, okay." Though this was the first time I had not washed my clothes at a town-stop, I didn't mind. It was a time-consuming chore, and my shirt smelled as bad coming out of town as it did going in.

Three days later I caught up with Aaron on the side of the trail as he was eating lunch. Because of the threat of winter storms, both of us had dropped off the Divide and were following the lower elevation Colorado Trail. Perusing our maps, we both noticed Princeton Hot Springs, fifteen miles southeast. We began musing over how great a hot spring would feel, having already labored twelve miles that morning. Our desire grew stronger with each comment, and soon we were shoveling down our lunch while hurriedly packing. We knew we would have to hustle to get there before they closed.

Aaron quickly left me behind, and then I passed him coming down a steep slope a few miles farther. He jumped ahead when I stopped to pee, and at the six-mile mark, I started jogging along the rocky trail as it contoured at 9,000 feet.

Miraculously, I caught him just as the trail ended at a parking area.

The town of Princeton waited four miles away in the heart of the valley. We settled into a brisk walk on tired feet and arrived in town a little after seven o'clock, and we had supper together.

We each ordered the only entrée under ten dollars, chicken fried steak, and together we ate five baskets of rolls before dinner arrived. Later we soaked in the hot tub until they closed at nine, then stumbled across the road to sleep in the open field at the center of town. We were up before dawn and on our way before anyone knew we were there.

Over the next four days, Aaron and I continued hiking together off and on. It was like being on vacation: sticking to the lower elevations, having someone to talk with and hitchhiking into Gunnison for pizza. Though we usually camped and ate together, we maintained our separate routines, rarely asking for or offering help. It felt companionable, yet free of many of the compromises that are a part of hiking with someone else.

Unfortunately, it would all come to an end soon. It was September 23rd. In two days I would reach Creede, the mining town where I had arranged to meet my friend, Anita Leahy. We had hiked together in the past and enjoyed each other's company, and I had invited her to join me through the San Juans. Now I almost regretted it.

Here I was reaching southern Colorado late in the season, and snow was a distinct possibility. Because of that, Aaron and I were hurrying right along. I knew that Anita had never hiked more than eleven miles in a single day. Aaron and I were averaging twenty-one. It would be difficult to alter my pace, which had become engrained over the past five months, and equally unreasonable to ask her to suddenly double her mileage. I hoped we could work out our different hiking paces, so I put it aside and thought about Greg.

He would be meeting me in Pagosa Springs to hike the final eighty-four miles together. Then my hike would be over. What had seemed like an endless summer had suddenly shrunk to a cramped few weeks. With a heavy heart I broke camp and waited for Aaron on the jeep road.

Finally! Another Thru-hiker
Silverthorne, CO south to San Luis Pass, CO

225

Blowing warmth into my hands, I surveyed the valley. To the south the road wound through sloping hills and gradually gained altitude as it headed deeper into the San Juan Mountains. Their peaks were snow-covered with what I hoped was just a dusting.

"What? You haven't raced off yet?" Aaron said as he came down the slope. He sounded pleased to see me.

"No." I waited until he was nearer. "I wanted to talk to you."

He stopped in front of me, a puzzled expression on his face. "What is it, Jen?"

"You know, my friend is going to be out in a couple of days. Then Greg will be back. Then my hike is over." My eyes pooled with emotion. Aaron looked away and adjusted his pack straps. "Anyway, I want to say goodbye here, Aaron. I need some time alone before I wind it up." I hesitated; afraid he would be hurt by what I said.

He hurried to reassure me: "Oh, yeah, no problem, I totally understand. I remember when I was finishing up the AT, it was tough. I didn't know why. I just needed to be alone." He started to hike backward down the trail. "Yeah, Jen, don't worry about it. Take it easy, all right?"

"Wait!" I cried, stunned by the suddenness of his departure.

I rushed forward and stopped. "Thanks for everything, Aaron. I wanted so badly to meet another thru-hiker, and, well, you know, it's been really great. Actually, I think this past eight days have been one of my favorite parts of the entire hike."

Lips pursed, Aaron looked down at me and took my hands in his. "Yeah, me, too," he murmured. Then we gave one another an awkward hug. "You take care of yourself," he said.

I nodded, and he was gone.

Chapter 16

Greg Returns for Hike's End
San Luis Pass, CO south to Chama, NM

I gave Aaron a ten minute head start then followed him up the valley. It felt wonderful to be alone again. It might not be for long, but at least I would have the San Juans all to myself for the next two days. I moved briskly up the trail, alert and attentive.

I hiked past a stand of lodgepole pines and turned east into the heart of the San Juan Mountains. Though the peaks were snow covered, I doubted the ridge would have more than a few inches of snow. I could wade through that easy enough. If a big storm hit, I would drop into the valley and hike along the highways. I hoped I wouldn't have to do that, but I was going to hike to Chama, New Mexico, one way or another.

That night I guessed that Aaron would camp at San Luis Pass; I stopped a couple of miles short of that and pitched my bivy sack amid a field of patchy brush.

I woke in the morning to find two inches of fresh snow covering the ridge. I scrambled out of my sleeping bag and stood in the silence. The sun strained to be seen through the thick fog, and the sounds of the nearby stream were muffled.

Fresh snow in the San Juan Mountains of southern Colorado made for slippery hiking and wet, cold feet. (Photo: Jennifer Hanson)

Refreshed and bursting with energy, I shook the ice and snow from my bivy sack and stuffed it into my pack. It was 7:30 a.m., and Spring Creek Pass was eighteen miles away. I hoped to reach it, hitch-hike forty-three miles into Creede and get to the Post Office before it closed at 4:30 p.m. It was going to be tight.

Trudging through the soft snow to the peak was easy, but once on the other side, the trail was frozen and slippery. It took an hour and a half to reach San Luis Pass. By then, Aaron was gone. Hiking up the far side, I found the unmistakable imprint of his tennis shoes. I smiled. Though I still wanted to hike alone, it was nice to know that he was on this snowy, 13,000 foot ridge with me. From the looks of it, we were the only ones.

When I reached the high ridge, I was stunned by the remarkable view. The sun had burned away the fog and created sparkles in the melting snow. I could see almost the entire San Juan Range, a horseshoe of snow-covered mountains with aspen and pine blanketing their slopes. The sky was a deep blue with puffy clouds drifting lazily above the Rio Grande Valley.

As the morning wore on, the snow melted, leaving the trail a wet mess. My boots were soaked and feet numb from the cold. I shed my jacket and hat and labored through the slush as I slipped on the muddy trail.

I wondered how Aaron's feet were doing. Because he wore only tennis shoes, he had even less protection from the cold. Then I remembered his Gore-Tex booties. His feet were probably warmer than mine. Lucky him!

I found where he stopped and turned, probably to check out the view and take a few pictures. I did the same. Later I noticed where he peed in the snow, and I felt embarrassed, as if I had caught him in the act.

A little after one o'clock, I rounded a cliff face of icy rock and stepped onto Snow Mesa. It was flat, featureless and covered with wet snow and large pools of water. It would take me all afternoon to cross its five mile expanse. I was tired of slipping in snow with wet, cold feet, but I had no choice. Look on the bright side, I teased myself; there was plenty of water to drink.

It was 3:30 in the afternoon when I reached the end of the plateau. The trail dropped swiftly through the pine trees, rocky and dry. Thrilled to be out of the slush, I held my pack tight to my back and jogged the last two miles to the highway. If I hurried, I might still make it to the Post Office in time.

As it turned out there was plenty of traffic, but no one stopped to give me a ride. Perhaps because each mile in the mountains was gained through such hard work, or because I knew that I, like most hikers, would do just about anything to help total strangers on the trail, but it seemed grossly selfish for drivers to not pick me up. It wasn't like I was asking them to personally carry me or my pack, apply first aid, or offer me the last of their food or water. All they had to do was sit on a soft cushiony seat, listen to their favorite tunes, adjust the temperature just right, exert a slight pressure to a gas pedal, and in no time at all arrive in Creede. Didn't they realize how easy they had it?

After twenty minutes of thumbing, a couple from out of town offered me a ride in the bed of their pick up. Speeding into the valley, the woman handed me chunks of pita bread through the window; I eagerly wolfed it down. They dropped me off at the Post Office at 4:35 p.m. It was closed.

Six days later I gathered my cooking supplies and glanced at my watch. It was 6:30 p.m., and I was waiting for my hiking friend, Anita, to catch up with me. It was our last day together, and we had decided we would camp near the natural hot springs that were marked on our map. We had covered most of the fifty-six miles from Creede to Highway 160 via South River Peak in the San Juan Mountains.

Five days earlier I would have sworn that hiking with Anita was a mistake in the making. At first I had forced myself to walk at her slower pace, but after a half-day of that I took off ahead of her in utter frustration and hiked alone. When I reached a confusing trail junction, I waited for her so she wouldn't get lost.

To my surprise, Anita wasn't upset that I had moved on. She was relaxed and seemed to be enjoying the hike more than when we were together with me silently pushing her onward. For the rest of the week I hiked my own hike, often leaving her behind in the process and waiting for her to catch up for meals and at the end of the day.

One last time I sat on a log and waited for Anita. I looked up through the pine trees and was taken by the beauty of their sunlit branches. Meanwhile, the temperature was dropping fast. Autumn was here, and in six days my hike would be over. I sighed. At least I would get to see Mom in Chama. She had decided to come after all. I remembered the letter I had gotten from her, telling me of her decision to make her first solo road trip. Underlining words to convey her pride and excitement, she had written:

I have started my list of what I want to pack on my trip!

Way to go, Mom, I thought. It was great to see her self-confidence rising. It wasn't like she hadn't always been capable of doing these things, but with Dad around, I doubt she had known it. Hell, she had raised ten kids while he was in Viet Nam, what couldn't she do?

Anita arrived, and I led her to the natural hot springs. Previous hikers had arranged walls of rocks to create two hot tubs on the bank of the river. I balanced my stove on the nearest ledge and put on a pot of curried rice and beans. Sinking back into the tub, I looked up past the canyon walls to the falling dusk.

I loved this part of the day, twilight, the time between the setting of the sun and the sighting of the first star. It had always felt mysterious to me and filled with promise. The wind died down, and the birds grew quiet. All I could hear was the hissing of the stove and the rippling of the stream.

I sat in my motel in Pagosa Springs; I was now waiting for Greg. Anita and I had said our goodbyes an hour earlier, and I was lounging in a chair, reading a magazine. Occasionally, I looked out the window, expecting him, expecting him, expecting him . . . I tried to imagine how it would feel to see him, to touch him, to smell him.

I dropped the magazine and picked up my gaiters. The rawhide strap had broken again and needed to be replaced. Before I finished, a truck pulled up, and there was Greg.

He stood beside the cab of the truck. He was wearing business slacks, a pressed shirt and loosened tie. He looked good, hadn't put on weight like I had expected. His hair was darker than I remembered, and he was grinning that priceless smile of his.

I ran to the door. "Need help with your stuff?" I called out.

He shook his head and pulled his bags from the truck. After dropping them in the room, he took off his tie and hugged me. It had been seven weeks, and it felt good: safe and familiar.

In the morning we left the truck for Art, my sister Linda's husband, to retrieve, then we hoisted our packs and hitchhiked a ride to Wolf Creek Pass at 10,857 feet. As the tiny Renault automobile in which we were riding labored up the mountain, the temperature dropped. Not good, I thought.

Thanking the driver, we stepped from the car and were engulfed in a thick, cold fog. At the edge of the parking lot was a large sign commemorating the Continental Divide National Scenic Trail, the first I had seen all summer. I shivered in front of it while Greg took my picture.

We stepped into the forest and were embraced by the scent of damp pine, and the higher I climbed, the better I felt. Reaching the top of the first ridge, I waited for Greg. Surprisingly, he wasn't far behind. I had insisted on carrying the bulk of our heavy gear; I wanted to protect his foot and give him time to acclimatize. Even so, I was amazed at how well he was doing.

I had to adjust to having Greg on the trail again. In the past seven weeks I had developed a fairly lean hiking style with little room for joking around. With Greg there, I often found myself wanting to hurry him or point out how he was wasting water or food.

One evening we stood beside a wind-bent fir, studying an open field of shrub grass and sandy soil. I handed the map back to Greg and pointed to where I thought we were.

He looked across the plateau and back the way we had come.

"Yeah, I think you're right, and according to Wolf's guidebook, there should be a stream at the end of this field. I've got to tell you, Jen, it's incredible how easy it is to follow his route," Greg said, thumping the mustard jacket of the Continental Divide Trail Society's guidebook. We had decided early in the hike not to carry the books in an effort to save weight, but on a whim, Greg had tossed one in his pack for this final leg. "I can't believe we didn't use these the entire way. They probably would have saved us a lot of headaches."

I had to agree but simply shrugged, my thoughts elsewhere.

"Honey," I said, "why don't we stop here for the night? I know it's a little early, but we're making good time, and that stream you mentioned sounds awfully nice."

He turned and smiled at me. "Oh, so you want to take it easy, do you? I was beginning to think I had married Rambo."

I shrugged and headed to the stream. He could tease me, but I was still going to keep us on track. The Southern San Juan Mountains in October were no place to dawdle.

We found a campsite, and I was carrying our water bottles to the stream when Greg asked, "Don't you think you should take your cup? The stream looks too shallow for the water bottle."

I stopped. He was right; I would be better off with the cup. He had probably saved me an extra trip on tired legs. Returning, I startled him with a sudden hug. "You know, Greg, that's the first time someone has looked out for me on the trail in almost two months."

He held me tighter.

"You just don't know, Greg, it's been so hard."

"I know, honey."

"No, you don't." I pushed away, suddenly angry. "Every minute of every day out here," I swept my arm wide to encompass the whole CDT, "constantly watching my step and the trail, the weather, my gear, how much water I'm drinking, animals, people, mileage. If I let down my guard for one minute, I could get caught in a storm or slip on a rock or get lost." I stood in front of him, shaking and bordering on tears. "It's

Our last day, October 6, Southern San Juan Mountains. Greg has returned for the finish of the hike. (Photo: Greg Allen)

been hard, Greg, really hard. *And you don't know.* You'll *never* know what it was like."

He watched me in silence, then he held open his arms. "You're right, Baby, you're right," he murmured into my hair. "But you're not alone anymore. I'm here."

For the first time since he left in August, I let go and really cried. Greg gently stroked my back until I pulled away to wipe my face dry.

Later, as I filled our water bottles, I marveled at how different I felt — as if I had come out of a war zone and was finally safe. The relief was huge, and yet I missed the intensity of my solo hike already. I wondered if my dad had felt this way when he came home from Nam: relieved, yet strangely empty, forced into a benevolent exile by living where so few really understood.

The morning of our last day on the trail broke clear and cold.

Coming off the ridge we were greeted by the rising sun, glistening off the frost covered sage. I snapped a picture of Greg's profile, beard half-formed and sleepy eyes filled with mist.

Throughout the morning I mentally recalled all that I loved about the trail, the sound and smell of the stove, the feeling of sinking into my sleeping bag, the call of an eagle, the smell of pine needles baking in the sun and sage drying after a rainfall. I treasured the creak of my pack swaying with each step, the sight of a long-sought stream, the howl of a coyote in the hours before dawn. I couldn't imagine how I could end this hike that I loved so well, how I could say goodbye.

I tried to think of the things I wouldn't miss: the barking of red squirrels, rain leaking through my jacket, being hungry all the time and the pain in my feet.

But it wasn't until I started to think of what I had to look forward to that my sadness began to lift. In Chama, I would get to see my mother, wear jeans and tennis shoes. Back in New York, I would drive a car and find a job. Eventually, we would buy a house, and someday I'd get pregnant again and have a baby. I pictured a little boy with dark, curly hair and chubby cheeks. That was definitely worth ending the hike for.

That afternoon the trail disappeared, and we spent a frustrating hour pursuing dead ends in an effort to find our route. We lost patience and abandoned all hope of following the map's trail; instead, we bushwhacked four miles straight through the woods. We relied solely on our instincts and dead reckoning, and we emerged from the trees and discovered a dirt road that was headed where we needed to go — east. Within a half-mile we came across two men building a fence. Greg watched our packs on the side of the road while I went to ask for directions.

"Can you tell me how to get to Cumbres Pass?"

"You're in Cumbres Pass," the first man answered.

"All right, can you tell me how to get to Highway Seventeen in Cumbres Pass?" I asked.

His companion, a Mexican, studied me for a minute, then began fishing through his wallet. Pulling out a card, he asked in a thick accent, "Are you Aaron Sheaffer's friend?"

"Oh my God, yes!"

"Are you Jennifer?"

"Yes! When did you see Aaron?"

He put the card carefully back into his wallet before answering. "He was here two, no, three days ago. He came out of the woods just where you did. Aaron said you would be here soon. He asked us to say hi."

I smiled and thanked them. Heading back to Greg, tears came to my eyes. It was like Aaron had been with me even when I couldn't see his footsteps and was miserably lost. Hell, he was probably lost too, I thought, smiling. Then he bushwhacked like we had, ending in the exact same spot. Perhaps we hadn't been lost at all but were exactly where we were supposed to be. To top matters, Aaron had known I would find my way, three days before I had lost it.

Excited, I told Greg what had happened. He was mildly impressed but mostly tired. We both were. It was two o'clock, and we had eight miles to go, most of that road walking. When we reached the highway, we found the pavement to be brutally hot and hard. After an hour of walking on it we still had three miles to go, and our spirits were low. I tried to convince Greg that being late wouldn't concern my family, but I didn't like being four hours behind schedule any more than he did. Besides, limping on the edge of a busy highway wasn't a very glamorous way to finish the hike.

"Greg, let's sing."

He started with my favorite song, "Me and Bobbie McGee," and my eyes welled up. It brought me back to our early days in New Mexico when we had the whole summer ahead of us. Looking back, I couldn't believe how much we had changed. I didn't feel like the same person who had set out six months before. It was hard to describe the difference, but it was as if I had begun this hike as a child — excited, naïve and

uncertain — and in the doing had become a woman — confident and
self-reliant.

By my best reckoning, I had hiked about 2,414 miles and Greg
had completed 1,600 miles. It had been six months and one week
since we began our trek, and in less than an hour it would be over.

We soon reached the outskirts of Chama. I looked ahead, then
called out, "There's Mom!"

She was in front of her motel across the street, waving and standing
tall and proud. She seemed elegant to me in her matching slacks and
top. My sister, Linda, hopped out of the car and joined her.

We hurried across the street and hugged them. In my fantasies of
this moment, I had often choked back tears. Now I was dry-faced and
calm. Maybe I was just exhausted and hungry, but in any event it
seemed anti-climactic.

We were greeted in Chama, New Mexico by my mother, Lois Hanson, and
sister, Linda Hanson. (Photo: someone passing by)

Greg Returns for Hike's End
San Luis Pass, CO south to Chama, NM
237

"It's over, Mom."

"Yes, dear, it is." She smiled at me and squeezed Greg's arm. "Let's get you two in a finishing photo."

Seeing her made me miss Dad even more. He would have been so pleased, so proud. Probably would have had a box of fudge or an ice cream cone waiting for us. I smiled sadly at the thought and wrapped my arm around Mom's waist in another hug.

Our pictures were taken, and still we milled about. There didn't seem much else to do; but, we were reluctant to leave, uncertain whether we had lived up to such a momentous occasion. Greg and I still had a mile to walk to the Chama River Bend Lodge — technically our end point — so we agreed to meet later for dinner and hugged them both goodbye.

And so, shortly, I lay on the motel bed while Greg stripped for his shower. We were staying in the same lodge that we had used when first arriving in New Mexico before the hike began, six months earlier. It was all so familiar and yet so different. Tomorrow we would be heading for the airport, not back to the trail.

"It doesn't seem real, Greg."

"It's going to feel real soon enough, Babe. By this time tomorrow we'll be back in New York." He smiled at me before heading into the shower.

I was surprised that I didn't feel more upset about ending the hike. But as I lay there with my feet in the air, soles pressed against the cool wall, I just felt a deep sense of accomplishment. It had been an amazing journey, nothing like I had imagined, yet so much more.

After dinner, Greg and I visited with my mother. Linda and Mom planned to leave early the next day to visit Mesa Verde, while Greg and I would head north to the Denver airport.

"So, Lois, how was your drive to Denver? I heard you were a little nervous about it," Greg said to my mother.

Her face lit up at his question, "Oh, it was wonderful. I was nervous like you said, but then decided I would simply do all the things I had seen Dad do in the past. I did, and everything turned out fine."

She was remarkable. She had no idea of the power she held. Here she was, alone for the first time in forty-six years. Instead of languishing in self-pity and fear, she was venturing out on her own — successfully.

"You know," she said with a smile that was almost smug, "Now that I made that trip, I feel like I could do anything I set my mind to."

Those could have been my words. Not wanting to detract from her moment, I smiled and thought to myself:

Me too, Mom, me too.

Eyes fixed on my goal, I cross a high rope bridge in Glacier National Park, Montana. (Photo: Greg Allen)

Appendix A

Thru-hike Preparation and Timeline

Preparing for a four to six month trek across the country is a major undertaking, but one that people have been doing for thousands of years. I suggest you give yourself a minimum of one year to prepare, but you can get away with less if you are an experienced long-distance hiker or can devote your full attention to the task.

Select a Trail

12–18 months prior to hiking: Pick a long-distance hike for your adventure. They each offer unique terrain, weather, popularity and degrees of remoteness. Take the time to research the alternatives and determine the right hike for you.

Contact Trail Associations

12–18 months: The best place to start is to review web sites of the varied trail associations that support and maintain the trails. For the CDT, use the Continental Divide Trail Alliance (CDTA) and Continental Divide Trail Society. *Backpacker* magazine's website also has a wealth of information, and there are numerous trail sites that allow you to read current thru-hikers' trail journals.

Develop Rough Itinerary

10–12 months: You need enough of an idea of your route so that you can start ordering maps and selecting supply points. We used the Continental Divide Trail Society's guidebook series as the foundation for our route, and I recommend it to others.

Save Money

12 months: Your maps alone can easily cost you $1,500. Other costs may include: light-weight equipment, clothing, food, traveler's checks in each supply box, the shipping of your supply boxes, and perhaps health insurance premiums and storage costs while you're hiking. We spent about $10,000 in 1997.

Get in Shape

12 months: Nothing prepares you for thru-hiking like actually thru-hiking that first month; however, it is wise to start getting in shape one year ahead. The purpose is to reduce the risk of injury, particularly early in the hike. Focus on strength, cardiovascular fitness and flexibility.

Research and Purchase Equipment

6–10 months: Don't leave this for the last minute. Your equipment will be your dearest possession and may even save your life in the not-so-distant future. Talk to friends, read the online equipment comparisons, research prices, make purchases and schedule a few outings to test it in the field.

Order Maps

6–10 months: Order a complete set of Map-Paks from the Continental Divide Trail Society. These maps correspond with Jim Wolf's guidebooks and include Trails Illustrated, Earthwalk Press, and National Forest maps. Once received, you will need to inventory them, create a list of additional maps needed (for areas the Map-Paks do not cover or for any deviations from the CDTS route that you plan to make). Be sure to order soon so you have your maps on hand to firm up your supply points. We also traced our intended route on state maps to better see the big picture. See Appendix E: Map List and Sources.

Hone Your Skills

2–8 months: Identify your weaknesses and start reading, practicing or taking courses on avalanche danger and ice-ax arrest, backcountry first aid, GPS/orienteering, and handling bears, cougars, rattlesnakes, lightning and river crossings.

Notify your Employer

6 months: Develop a realistic plan about missing 4–6 months of work, and notify your employer early when appropriate. Give some thought to how you'll be covered for health insurance, and if/how you will store your possessions while away.

Identify Mail Drops

5–7 months: Estimate the number of miles you'll hike per day, the weight of your food per day and how many days worth of food you can carry. This will give you a rough idea of how frequently you should schedule your mail drops. Review the maps, firm up your itinerary and make your picks. Then contact any that are not a Post Office. Make sure these private resorts still accept thru-hiker packages and that you have the correct address.

Buy and Pack Food

3–4 months: Keep it simple. Pick 3–4 meals that you like and stock up. You'll get variety in town so shouldn't become too bored. I highly recommend freeze-dried food; it is light, nutritious and delicious. But be prepared for those nights you can't find water. Nearly every small town in America has a convenience store where you can stock up on nuts, candy bars, cereal, beef jerky, peanut butter and pasta. Save on postage and add variety to your menu by purchasing those along the way. Don't forget the first aid kit.

Mail Drop Support

3–4 months: Who will mail your packages to you? Find someone who is meticulous about deadlines. You don't want to be stuck in a small town without your maps, food and traveler's checks. Be sure they have a dry, rodent free place to store your mail boxes. When you deliver your boxes to their care they should be clearly addressed and left open so that changes can be made up to the day they are mailed. Your mail drop person should be kept well informed of your progress and any changes in itinerary.

Compile Phone Number List

1–3 months: Compile a lightweight list of phone numbers and/or addresses (or email addresses) for friends, family, equipment manufacturers, local forest ranger or BLM staff, non-Post Office mail drops, and National Park Backcountry Offices.

Get a Tan

0–3 months: Visit a tanning booth so you're not at the mercy of the sun. Try to squeeze in a few short backpacking trips or at least load your pack with books, put on your new boots and start walking or using the StairMaster. The more you break in now, the less miserable you will be your first month on the trail.

Say Goodbye

0–1 week: Congratulations. You have completed your preparations and it is time to go. Say your goodbyes and head to the trail. You are about to embark on one of the greatest adventures of your life!

Appendix B

Equipment and Clothing List

Key

A — Always Carried
R — Returned Nonessential
D — Desert
S — Snow and Mountains
G — Returned After Greg Left
J — Jen Hiking Alone

Personal Equipment	Key
backpack (Dana Design)	A
backpack pouch w/water bottle	A
backpack raincover	A
0F down sleeping bag w/sack	A
-length sleeping pad (SI)	A
1 large black trash bag	A
1 qt water bottle (Nalgene)	R
micro headlamp (Petzl)	G
1-battery flashlight	J
knife (Leatherman)	G
1-oz single blade knife	J
compass	A

datapouch   R
whistle and carabineer   A
snowshoes (Redfeather/Atlas)   S
trekking poles (Leki)   A
pepper spray (small can)   S
camera, film, spare batteries   A
solar AA-battery recharger   R
toothbrush,TP, wipes,deodorant   A

Shared Equipment   **Key**

15 oz tarp   D
2-person non-freestanding tent   S,G
tent ground cover   S,G
bivy sack (Moonstone)   J
multi-fuel stove (Apex II)   A
° qt. fuel bottle w/fuel   A
1 pot w/lid, handle, matches   A
2 plastic cups & spoons   A
BakePacker (pot & lid)   R
water pump   G
2.5 and 1.0 liter water bags   G
9 oz GPS (Garmen)   A
altimeter watch   A
50 ft spectra rope   G
3 oz parachute cord   J
first aid & repair kits   A
candle lantern   R
maps, pen & paper   A
money, ID, addresses/phone #s   A

Equipment Repair Kits   Key

replacement stove parts	A
sleeping pad repair kit	A
thread, needles, safety pins	A
duct tape (on fuel bottle)	A
spare trekking pole tips	R

First Aid Kit   Key

ibuprofen	A
broad-spectrum antibiotics	A
iodine tablets-water treatment	A
antibiotic ointment	A
antacid and antihistamine	A
small & large Band-Aids	A
micro-pore tape, sterile pads	A
scissors and tweezers	A
moleskin	A
sun & lip screen (Dermatone)	A
Ace bandage	A

Clothes Jen & Greg Carried   Key

mesh bag for clothes	A
1 pr hiking socks	A
1 pr liner socks	R
1 pr warm hiking socks	S
sandals (Teva) / flip-flops	A
spare running shorts	R
spare singlet w/sleeves	R
long sleeve synthetic shirt	A
fleece sweater	A
polypropolene long johns (2 pair)	A

bra, tampons, pads	A
fleece hat	A
glove liners	A
jacket (Gore-Tex)	A
gloves (Gore-Tex)	S
wind pants	A

Clothing Worn While Hiking	**Key**
boots (Merrill Light)	D
full-leather boots (Scarpa)	S
hiking socks	A
liner socks	R
polypro short-sleeve shirt	A
running shorts	A
hat with brim	A
sunglasses with strap	A
gaiters	A
watch	A
bandana	A

Appendix C

Food List

On the following pages are two lists of what we typically ate on the trail. The first list is for a five-day leg at the beginning of the hike (with Greg) and the second list is from the end of my hike (alone).

Freeze-dried food made meals enjoyable, nutritious, light and affordable. Adventure Foods did a great job for us. They can be reached at (828) 497-4113, www.adventurefoods.com.

Every supply town has a convenience store where you can purchase cereal, pasta, nuts, beef jerky, peanut butter and snacks. Save postage, add variety to your menu and support local economies by purchasing these items along the way.

Mayonnaise packets, like the small ones you find at a deli, become cooking oil once heated. No refrigeration is required, and they don't become rancid.

The wax-covered cheese in our food drops only worked for the first month. After that they exploded and made a mess of everything.

Initially, we carried Gatorade powder and hot chocolate, fearing we would become bored with water. We discovered that it was just too heavy, and, besides, water is delicious!

Food Carried for Jen & Greg (5-day leg)   Total Weight (oz.)

Staples:

butter powder	4
powdered milk	12
powdered eggs	4
hot cocoa powder	16
assorted herbal teas	0
whole wheat flour	12
white flour	4
Bisquick mix	4
Gatorade powder	8
iced tea powder	4
cheddar cheese powder	6
Monterey Jack cheese	12
Parmesan cheese	4
mayonnaise packets (oil)	2
assorted spices	3
pepperoni	16
ramen noodle soup	5

Snacks:

granola bars / fruit bars	16
M&M's / power bars	6
party mix	12
raisins	8
dried fruit	4
rice / oat / popcorn cakes	6
mixed nuts	12

Deserts:

pudding/Pop-Tarts/cheesecake	8

Breakfasts:

oatmeal & granola	10
dehydrated hash browns	4
dry cereal	8
powdered potatoes	12

Dinners:

assorted pasta	20
freeze-dried lentils	4
black beans, pinto beans	4
cous-cous	6
precooked dehydrated brown rice	8
polenta	4
freeze-dried beef	3
freeze-dried chicken	3
freeze-dried vegetables	6
tomato powder	4
sliced potatoes	4

TOTAL WEIGHT:	18 lb

Food Carried for Jen alone (5-day leg)	**Total Weight (oz.)**

Snacks:

candy bars (2/day)	20
hard candy	8

Breakfast:

powdered milk	5
dry cereal	16

Lunch (1oz. package each):

beef jerky	5

cheese crackers	5
Spanish peanuts	5

Dinner:

pasta w/fd beef, veggies, and tomato powder	21
freeze-dried lentils, rice, chicken, veggies, curry	12

Spice Baggies:

salt, pepper, garlic powder, curry, and cinnamon	3

TOTAL WEIGHT: **6.3 lb.**

Appendix D

Itinerary and Supply Points

This itinerary, and the map list in Appendix E, are from our 1997 hike. The Continental Divide Trail has gone through numerous changes since then and will continue to evolve in the years to come. Updated map lists, mail drop locations, and land manager contacts for the official trail can be found on the Continental Divide Trail Alliance website at www.cdtrail.org.

The hike we made can be viewed below. The listings include supply box numbers, arrival dates, locations, supply box mailing addresses and ranger stations/national parks contact info (current as of July 2009), miles to TH (trail head), hiked miles and total miles.

Box #	Arrival Date	Location	Supply Box Mailing Address GD = General Delivery	Ranger Station National Park (NP) RD = Ranger District NF = National Forest	Mi. to TH	Hiked Miles	Total Miles
	Apr 1	Mexican Border @ Columbus, NM	Start of Hike!				
1	Apr 3	Deming, NM	GD Deming, NM 88030 (575) 546-9461	NM BLM State Office & Santa Fe NF (505) 438-7400	0	38	38
2	Apr 9	Pinos Altos, NM	GD, Silver City, NM 88061 (505) 538-2831	Silver City RD, Gila NF (575) 388-8201	7	100	138

Box #	Arrival Date	Location	Supply Box Mailing Address GD = General Delivery	Ranger Station/ National Park (NP) RD = Ranger District NF = National Forest	Mi. to TH	Hiked Miles	Total Miles
3	Apr 16	Reserve, NM	GD, Reserve, NM 87830 (575) 533-6333	Reserve RD, Gila NF (575) 533-6232	0	106	244
4	Apr 21	Quemado, NM	GD Quemado, NM 87829	Quemado RD, Gila NF (575) 773-4678	0	71	315
5	Apr 26	Grants, NM	GD, Grants, NM 87020 (505) 287-3143	NW NM Visitors Ctr. (505) 876-2783 Mt. Taylor RD, Cibola NF (505) 287-8833	0	99	414
6	May 2	Cuba, NM	GD Cuba, NM 87013 (505) 744-6790	Cuba RD, Santa Fe NF (575) 289-3264 Cuba BLM Field Off. (575) 289-3748	0	102	516
7	May 6	Ghost Ranch Conf. Center, NM	Ghost Ranch CC HC 77, Box 11 Abiquiu, NM 87510 (505) 685-4333	Santa Fe NF 1474 Rodeo Rd. Santa Fe, NM 87505 (505) 438-7400	0	56	572
8	May 10	Chama, NM	Chama River Bend Lodge, Hwy 84, Rte. 1, Chama, NM 87520 (505) 756-2264	Carson NF 208 Cruz Alta Rd. Taos, NM 87571 (575) 758-6200	13	84	656
	May 14	South Pass, WY	Begin Second Leg				
9	May 19	Wamsutter, WY	GD, Wamsutter, WY 82336 (307) 324-3764	BLM Casper District Office 1701 East E St. Casper, WY 82604 (307) 261-7600	0	87	743
10	May 24	Encampment, WY	GD Encampment, WY 82325 (307) 327-5747	Brush Creek/ Hayden RD, Medicine Bow-Routt NF, Encampment, WY 82325 (307) 326-5258	0	92	835

11	May 29	Steam-boat Springs, CO	GD Steamboat Springs, CO 80477 phone (970) 870-3001	Hahns Peak/Bears Ear RD, Medicine Bow-Routt NF (970) 879-1870 Rocky Mountain National Park (970) 586-1242	10	63	898
12	June 10	Silver-thorne, CO	GD, Silverthorne, CO 80498 (970) 513-1629			0	147	1,045
	June 29	Warm Springs, MT		Begin Third Leg			
13	July 5	Lincoln, MT	GD, Lincoln, MT 59410 (406) 362-4523	Lincoln RD, Helena NF (406) 362-4265	19	118	1,163
14	July 19	Bench-mark Wilder-ness Ranch, MT	Benchmark Wilderness Ranch, 422 County Line Rd., Fairfield, MT 59436 (406) 467-3110	Flathead NF 1935 - 3rd Ave., E. Kalispell, MT 59901 (406) 758-5204	0	52	1,215
15	July 24	East Glacier Park, MT	GD, East Glacier Park, MT 59434 (406) 226-5534	Glacier National Park (406) 888-7800	0	128	1,343
	Aug 2	Warm Springs, MT		Begin Fourth Leg			
16	Aug 2	Anaconda, MT	GD Anaconda, MT 59711 (406) 563-2241	Butte RD, Beaverhead-Deerlodge NF (406) 494-2147	0	9	1,352
17	Aug 10	Wisdom, MT	GD Wisdom, MT 59761 (406) 689-3224	Wisdom RD, Beaverhead-Deerlodge NF (406) 689-3243	25	90	1,442
18	Aug 17	Leadore, ID	GD, Leadore, ID 83464 (208) 768-2285	Leadore RD, Salmon-Challis NF (208) 768-2500	13	124	1,566

Box #	Arrival Date	Location	Supply Box Mailing Address GD = General Delivery	Ranger Station/ National Park (NP) RD = Ranger District NF = National Forest	Mi. to TH	Hiked Miles	Total Miles
19	Aug 24	Mack's Inn, ID	Mack's Inn Resort PO Box 10, Mack's Inn, ID 83433 (208) 558-7272	Island Park RD, Caribou-Targhee NF (208) 558-7301 Yellowstone NP (307) 344-2160/ 2164	0	114	1,680
20	Aug 30	Togwotee Lodge, WY	Togwotee Mountain Lodge PO Box 91, Hwy 26 & 287 South, Jackson Hole, WY 83013 (866) 278-4245	Bridger-Teton NF (307) 739-5500	2	119	1,799
21	Sep 6	Big Sandy Lodge, WY	Big Sandy Lodge 8 Spotted Tail Circle, Rock Springs, WY 82901 (307) 382-6513	Wind River RD, Shoshone NF (307) 455-2466	2	149	1,948
22	Sep 8	South Pass, WY	GD, Lander, WY 82520 (307) 332-3282	Pinedale RD Bridger-Teton NF (307) 367-4326	35	53	2,001
	Sep 11	Silver-thorne, CO	Begin Fifth Leg				
23	Sep 14	Twin Lakes, CO	GD Twin Lakes, CO 81251	Leadville RD, Pike & San Isabel NF (719) 486- 0749	0	76	2,077
24	Sep 17	Salida, CO	GD, Salida, CO 81201 (719) 539-2548	Salida RD, Pike & San Isabel NF (719) 539-3591	18	65	2,142
25	Sep 25	Creede, CO	GD, Creede, CO 81130 (719) 658-2615	Divide RD, Rio Grande NF (719) 658-2556	9	111	2,253

26	Oct 2	Pagosa Springs, CO	GD, Pagosa Springs, CO 81147 (970) 264-5440	Pagosa RD, San Juan NF (970) 264-2268	23	92	2,345
	Oct 6	Chama, NM		End of Hike		69	2,414

Appendix E

Map List and Sources

Key:
- BLM   Bureau of Land Management
- CT   Colorado Trail
- EP   Earthwalk Press
- FS   U.S. Forest Service
- TI   Trails Illustrated
- USGS   United States Geological Society

Box #	Location	Maps Carried	Map Maker	
	Mexican Border	Columbus, NM	BLM	
		Deming, NM	BLM	
1	Deming, NM	Hatch, NM	BLM	
		Gila National Forest		FS
3	Reserve, NM	Quemado, NM	BLM	
4	Quemado, NM	Cibola National Forest, Mt. Taylor Dis.	FS	
		Acoma Pueblo, NM	BLM	
		Fence Lake, NM	BLM	
		Zuni, NM	BLM	
		Grants, NM	BLM	
5	Grants, NM	Chaco Mesa, NM	BLM	
		Chaco Canyon, NM	BLM	
6	Cuba, NM	Abiquiu, NM	BLM	
		Santa Fe National Forest	FS	

7	Ghost Ranch Conference Center, NM	Chama, NM	BLM
		Carson National Forest	FS
		CDT Rio Grande #1	FS
		South San Juan Wilderness Area #142	TI
		Antonito, CO	BLM
8	Chama, NM (start of 2nd leg)	South Pass, WY	BLM
		Red Desert Basin, WY	BLM
		Rawlins, WY	BLM
		Lander, WY	BLM
		Bairoil, WY	BLM
9	Wamsutter, WY	Baggs, WY	BLM
		Medicine Bow National Forest	FS
10	Encampment, WY	Hahns Peak, Steamboat Lake #116	TI
		Clark, Buffalo Pass #117	TI
11	Steamboat Springs, CO	Steamboat Springs, Rabbit Ears #118	TI
		Rand, Stillwater Pass #115	TI
		Rocky Mtn Natl Park #200	TI
		Indian Peaks, Gold Hill #102	TI
		Arapaho & Roosevelt Natl. Forests	FS
		Winter Park, Rollins Pass #103	TI
		Idaho Springs, Loveland Pass #104	TI
		Vail, Frisco, Dillon #108	TI
		White River National Forest	FS
12	Silverthorne, CO (start of 3rd leg)	Deerlodge National Forest	FS
		Helena National Forest	FS
		Thunderbolt Creek	USGS
		Bison Mountain	USGS
		MacDonald Pass	USGS
		Greenhorn Mountain	USGS
13	Lincoln, MT	Bob Marshall Wilderness Area	FS
14	Benchmark Wilderness Ranch, MT	Glacier National Park #215	TI
16	Anaconda, MT (start of 4th leg)	Anaconda-Pintlar Wilderness	FS
		Bitterroot National Forest	FS
		Shultz Saddle	USGS
		Lost Trail Pass	USGS

continued on the next page

Box #	Location	Maps Carried	Map Maker
17	Wisdom, MT	Salmon National Forest	FS
		Homer Youngs Peak	USGS
		Miner Lake	USGS
		Goldstone Pass	USGS
		Kitty Creek	USGS
		Lemhi Pass	USGS
		Goat Mountain	USGS
		Bannock Pass	USGS
18	Leadore, ID	Targhee — East & West	FS
		Deadman Pass	USGS
		Tepee Mountain	USGS
		Island Butte	USGS
		Eighteenmile Peak	USGS
		Deadman Lake	USGS
		Gullagher Gulch	USGS
		Lima Peaks	USGS
		Snowline	USGS
		Monida	USGS
		Corral Creek	USGS
		Big Table Mountain	USGS
		Lower Red Rock Lake SW	USGS
		Lower Red Rock Lake SE	USGS
		Upper Red Rock Lake	USGS
		Mount Jefferson	USGS
19	Mack's Inn, ID	Buffalo Lake NE	USGS
		Latham Spring	USGS
		Old Faithful	TI
		Yellowstone Lake	TI
		Bridger-Teton National Forest	FS
20	Togwotee Lodge, WY	North Wind River Range	EP
		South Wind River Range	EP
21	Big Sandy Lodge, WY	South Pass, WY	BLM
22	Silverthorne, CO (start of 5th leg)	Breckenridge, Tennessee Pass #109	TI
		Holy Cross, Ruedi Reservoir #126	TI
		Aspen, Independence Pass #127	TI
		San Isabel National Forest	FS
		Gunnison Basin Wilderness Area	FS
		Colorado Trail Index	CT
		Colorado Trail maps #5—12	CT

23	Twin Lakes, CO	Buena Vista, Collegiate Peaks #129	TI
		Crested Butte, Pearl Pass #131	TI
		Salida, St. Elmo, Shavano Peak #130	TI
		Colorado Trail maps #13—16	CT
24	Garfield, CO	La Garita Wilderness #139	TI
		Silverton, Telluride, Lake City #141	TI
		Weminuche Wilderness #140	TI
		Rio Grande National Forest	FS
		Colorado Trail maps #17—24	CT
25	Creede, CO	South San Juan Wilderness #142	TI
		San Juan	FS
		CDT Scenic Trail #7 — Rio Grande	FS
26	Pagosa Springs, CO	Antonito, CO	BLM
		CDT Scenic Trail #2—6 Rio Grande	FS
		CDT Scenic Trail #1 Rio Grande	FS

MAP SOURCES

Continental Divide Trail Society

www.cdtsociety.org

Guidebooks — A series of buidebooks which include: a detailed description of the Continental Divide Trail; descriptive text listing mileages to important features; charts providinig section mileage and elevation gains; lists of relevant USGS maps; and, overview maps at a scale of ° inch to the mile.

Map-Paks — A set of maps that correspond with each of the CDTS guidebooks. They include Trails Illustrated, Earthwalk Press, and Forest Service maps, as well as photocopied maps to cover some of the missed sections.

Public Lands Information Center: Map Center

http://plicmapcenter.org

BLM   1:100,000 scale; contour intervals 50 m; lat./long.; towns, roads, water sources including windmills and stock tanks. Quite reliable.

FS   1:126,720 scale; no contour lines; lat./long.; spot elevations; towns, roads, some water sources. Roads/trails may be inaccurate or outdated, nonetheless, these maps provide big picture and were at times the only maps we used.

United States Geological Society
http://topomaps.usgs.gov
(888) 275-8747

USGS   1:25,000 scale; contour intervals 40 ft.; lat./long.; excellent detail of roads, water sources. Such small scale you walk off the map within hours. Only recommend these in cases where FS 1:126,720 maps are all that are available.

USGS maps are also available through many commercial sites, including www.offroute.com, www.trails.com or www.MyTopo.com.

Trails Illustrated
www.cdtrail.org — Continental Divide Trail Alliance

TI   1:40,680 scale; contour intervals 40 ft.; lat./long.; excellent maps. Recommended where available.

Earthwalk Press
2239 Union Street
Eureka, CA 95501
(800) 828-6277
www.cdtrail.org — Continental Divide Trail Alliance

EP   1:48,000 scale; contour interval 40 ft.; no lat./long. or UTM; otherwise reliable, detailed maps.

Colorado Trail
www.coloradotrail.org — The Colorado Trail Foundation

CT   1:25,000 scale; detailed topo maps with UTM, lat./long. and GPS waypoints available at reasonable price.

Index

About the Author

Jennifer A. Hanson was born in Heidelberg, Germany in 1959 while her father was stationed there with the U.S. Army. She graduated from the United States Military Academy at West Point, New York in 1981 and became an avid back-packer and outdoorswoman.

In addition to thru-hiking the 2,414-mile Continental Divide Trail, Jennifer has completed the northern third of the Appalachian Trail, most of Vermont's Long Trail, back-packed in the Canadian Rockies and has climbed to the highest point in a dozen states across the country.

She has been employed as an Appalachian Trail Ridge Runner and has served as a Local Hike Reporter for www.LocalHikes.com. Her website, www.HikingtheCDT.com, offers tips for hikers as well as more photographs and anecdotes from her CDT thru-hike.

Jennifer also enjoys snow-shoeing and alpine skiing, and delights in teaching these skills to others, especially youngsters. She is the owner of Hanson Financial Services, a computer consulting company, and lives in upstate New York with her partner, Denise Watso, and their two children.